EXPLORING
YELLOWSTONE

Exploring Yellowstone

By RUTH KIRK

Photographs by Ruth and Louis Kirk

Published in cooperation with
Yellowstone Library and Museum Association
by the University of Washington Press
Seattle and London

Copyright © 1972 by the University of Washington Press
Printed in the United States of America

Library of Congress Cataloging in Publication Data

Kirk, Ruth.
    Exploring Yellowstone.

    Bibliography: p.
    1. Yellowstone national park. I. Title.
F722.K5   917.87'52'043   78–178702
ISBN 0–295–95174–5
ISBN 0–295–95188–5 (pbk.)

Photographs by Ruth and Louis Kirk except pp. 14 and 15, courtesy Yellowstone National Park Museum Archives; p. 19, courtesy Historical Society of Montana, Helena. Maps and drawings by Yoshi Nishihara

PREFACE

Throughout the world the name Yellowstone is recognized. To most people in the United States it means Old Faithful and Mammoth Terrace and bears —and summer crowds. Abroad, the name symbolizes open, wild country and the foresight of a young nation in setting aside pristine land as a national park, the first in the world. Perhaps the foreign viewpoint comes closer to the truth than our own for a simple reason: when we are in Yellowstone its spectacles seem a sufficiency in themselves. The eye and mind are absorbed and feel no urge to explore beyond the obvious. Yet the park is vast, reaching far, far beyond its looping roads. And it is diverse. The awesome sculpture of the Canyon, a yellow gash that stretches for twenty-six miles, would be reason for a park in itself; so would Yellowstone Lake, huge, blue, wild, home of nesting pelicans and swans and ospreys. So would the herds of elk and the buffalo, deer, moose, bighorn sheep, antelope, grizzly bears, coyotes, wolves—wildlife not unlike that of the great African preserves in abundance and natural freedom.

The simple fact of the park's existence carries great significance in itself. Here the rhythms that rocked the wilderness cradle still linger. Here scientists —newly and urgently involved with understanding environment—can find an intact sample of the primeval, and through continual observation can update their findings and postulations. Here the individual can stretch his soul.

It is my hope that this book will guide both the mind and the feet in exploring the park. Material drawn upon has included innumerable published and unpublished sources, plus the generous help and criticism of specialists. To all, my awareness of debt and my gratitude. Material has come also from repeated trips to the park, and to those who shared roads and trails and canoeways go fond memories of a pink dawn at Mammoth Terrace, of fishing in Slough Creek, waiting out wind on Shoshone Lake, watching elk by the hundreds along the Firehole River, and standing silent as Old Faithful filled the night with its spectral plume.

> *The wonder of the world,*
> *The beauty and power, the shapes of things,*
> *their colours, lights and shades;*
> *These I saw.*
> *Look ye also, while life lasts.*
> —From an old English tombstone

RUTH KIRK

CONTENTS

The Human Story

Yellowstone in winter

EARLY DAYS

Yellowstone spreads across the rooftree of the continent as a series of high plateaus with meadows and lodgepole pine forests and rolling sage flats; a land of river headwaters and a vast lake sparkling and blue in summer, frozen white in winter, and swept by winds the year around.

Add to this picture bubbling mudpots, hot springs, geysers steaming like smoke from a thousand fires, mountains belching out water hot enough to reverse the green advance of grasses and trees, and gases so noxious they kill songbirds. Add also wildlife—buffalo whose running shakes the ground, swans and sandhill cranes whose trumpeting carries like the brass of a symphony orchestra. And add man, beginning eleven or twelve thousand years ago as the most recent of the earth's successive ice ages was at last relinquishing its sterile grip.

TRACING THE PAST

Lance points of the Clovis type are found in Montana, and Folsom points are fairly common in eastern Montana and Wyoming, appearing as close to Yellowstone as Gardiner, barely north of the park, and in the Gros Ventre Mountains, slightly south of the park. Both types of points date back more than ten millennia to early hunters who roamed after herds of large mammals and killed as they had need and opportunity. Clovis points always lie associated with mammoth kills; Folsom points, with bison kills. Neither type is an "arrowhead," for the bow and arrow were not developed until about thirty-five hundred years ago, and were introduced into the Yellowstone area only about seventeen hundred years ago. Early hunters used short spears which they hurled with special throwing sticks for leverage.

When the ice age closed, the entire mid-continent became much hotter and drier than it had been, or is now. By about 5000 B.C. mammoths and giant bison, the ancestors of today's buffalo, had vanished from the plains, possibly because of the climate change, possibly hunted to extermination by man; nobody knows. With food gone and the plains baked by heat and drought, man's life patterns changed. Hunters shifted to the pursuit of elk and deer and rabbits in uplands such as Yellowstone where high plateaus remained as refuges of relative coolness and moisture—green havens with fish in the rivers and animals still grazing meadows. Families and bands from the Great Basin, already experienced in living off small game and arid-land plants,

3

now also moved to the Yellowstone region to escape the growing heat of their previous territory.

About 1000 B.C. the climate moderated. Herds of buffalo and elk again massed on the plains outside Yellowstone as well as on ranges within the park, and again man adapted to meet new economic opportunities. The patterns of Indian life reported by the first European explorers began to be established. The Yellowstone region, headwaters for the Madison, Yellowstone, and Snake rivers, was long supposed to have acted as a buffer zone—a geographic barrier—between the different cultures surrounding the park area. Recent evidence, however, testifies to a mixing of cultures. Yellowstone became a meeting ground as bands traveled there for pigments or obsidian or other resources not readily plentiful elsewhere.

To the east and north were the Plains tribes—Crows and Blackfeet—people who lived vigorously and well by hunting buffalo. To the northwest were the Flatheads, adapted to intermontane life. At times the hunters from these tribes entered the park. Circles of stones that may once have snugged the bottoms of their tipi skins to the ground (or that may date from an earlier time) are known near Obsidian Cliff and along Blacktail Deer Creek and Slough Creek. Some measure twenty feet in diameter. There are also lines of stones piled into walls as much as seventy-five yards long—corrals into which buffalo and possibly elk were driven for slaughter. Such walls have been found with projectile points close by, along with animal bones showing butchering marks and stone scrapers used in preparing hides. Outside the park, "jumps" that served the same purpose as the corral walls are frequent along the Madison, Gallatin, and Yellowstone rivers. The technique was to stampede the beasts over a cliff, sometimes by setting fires to force herds into mass, frenzied motion and sometimes by creeping among them dis-

Buffalo herd

Bighorn sheep

guised in wolf or antelope skins, then standing and spooking them. Sentinels posted for miles along the intended path of the stampede would shout and wave robes to spur on the crazed herd.

West of Yellowstone were Shoshone and Bannock Indians, tribes that hunted bighorn sheep. In the park they added fish to their diet, as indicated by stone net sinkers found along the shores of Yellowstone Lake. They may also have gathered eggs from the gull and pelican rookeries on the islands, and stone mortars and pestles found at scattered campsites imply use of seeds, berries, and roots.

LAST DAYS

The only Indians living the year around in the park area when white men first arrived were the Tukudika (also spelled "Dukurika"), or Sheepeaters. These were satellite Shoshone and Bannock Indians who had no horses or guns and so found it hard to keep up with the fast-paced, affluent life of the Plains peoples. Some Tukudika had probably arrived from the west centuries earlier, already accustomed to life as gatherers of plants and hunters of small game. Others seem to have been impoverished families who retreated to the simple, subsistence-level life of the high Yellowstone country. The name "Sheepeater" comes from their staple diet, bighorn sheep; other Indians, outside the park, were called Buffalo Eaters and Antelope Eaters.

The Tukudikas' system was to follow bands of sheep into the mountains, taking along large dogs to pack out the meat and hides on travoises. Obsidian tools served for butchering and skinning, and despite early reports disparaging Tukudika tools, which tended to be crude, the fact is that stone blades can function surprisingly well. In a recent test by anthropologists, knives flaked from obsidian and tested in skinning a cow held their edge better than steel hunting knives.

In addition to sheep, the Tukudikas hunted elk and deer by building barriers of saplings and fallen timber to channel the animals' movement and increase the effectiveness of hunting from blinds. One such driveway reported by an early park superintendent had wings that reached from Swan Lake to the pine groves at the base of Sheepeater Cliff. The focal point was a blind near Rustic Falls, at the head of today's Golden Gate road above Mammoth.

In addition to the Tukudikas, one band of Wyoming Shoshone sometimes wintered near the southeast corner of Yellowstone when hunger made them desperate, from there pushing on snowshoes into the heartland of the park to hunt elk and sheep and beaver. They also came to trade with the Tukudikas for sheep horn and hide, to fish at Yellowstone Lake, and to rest and cure themselves at various hot springs. Even after removal to the Wind River Reservation, Shoshones returned to Yellowstone each summer to hunt and fish.

After the 1840s when buffalo herds on the western plains had been eliminated, Bannock Indians began to make yearly crossings of Yellowstone, traveling from the Snake River Plains to the rolling prairie east of the park where the last of the great herds still ran free. The trek led for two hundred miles, a wearisome journey for families, but worth the cost because the promise of buffalo beef and hides was better than the alternative of life reduced to the endless foraging of desert peoples. For forty years the Bannocks made their treks, from 1838 to 1878, rutting the earth so deeply with their horse travoises that the marks can still be traced across the park, most easily in the Tower Falls area.

A few scattered, half-standing wickiups speak today of these journeys, or perhaps of lone families that wandered into Yellowstone in the last days to forestall surrender to reservation life. Best preserved are a pair on the edge of the Gallatin Valley just outside the park. The larger is formed of 150 poles—a lodge ten feet wide inside and providing shelter because of its many poles, even without a covering of skins. The setting close to a creek suggests a summer hunting or fishing camp. Other wickiups are on Lava Creek, east of Mammoth.

INDIAN REACTION TO THERMAL BASINS

White men associated with Yellowstone from the first *voyageurs* to the early park administrators claimed that Indians shunned the thermal basins, but recent archaeological evidence runs counter to this. The contention had been that, although hot springs elsewhere served medicinally or as places of sacred refuge, the magnitude of Yellowstone's hissing and steaming made it too awesome to approach.

Lewis and Clark heard no detail of the region's wonders from the Indians they encountered on their journey to the Pacific. Their journal simply mentions hearing of a "considerable falls" on the upper Yellowstone River. Early trappers also reported that Indian guides were knowledgeable about the wilderness around Yellowstone, but knew little of the peculiar phenomena within the boundaries of today's park. There were Indian trails, the trappers said, but they showed little use and as often as not were half overgrown. Father DeSmet, a missionary, corroborated this view on the basis of a trip in 1851 from the mouth of the Yellowstone River to Fort Laramie, on the Platte. "The Indians speak of [Yellowstone] with a superstitious fear," he wrote in a letter, "and consider it the abode of evil spirits, that is to say, a kind of hell. [They] seldom approach it without offering some sacrifice, or, at least, without presenting the calumet of peace to the turbulent spirits, that they may be propitious."

Doubtless there was basis for the reports. Some Plains Indians must have feared the thermal regions and stayed away; but clearly others sought spirit power there, or came to hunt the animals congregated around the geysers in winter because of warmth and snow-free ground. Species from buffalo to geese still graze the riverbanks and meadows of the thermal basins, and archaeologists have found artifacts and chips there, some scattered on the timbered knobs surrounding geyser and hot spring areas, some out on the sinter, even close to vents. One archaeologist described a find lying on a thermal dome that "continually shuddered and vibrated [so much] I felt it might collapse or blow out at any time." Crude vermillion (ocher) and pure sulphur evidently had been dug at this same site, near Trout Creek, both probably used as pigment and the sulphur perhaps also valued as medicine. Similar sites have been found at Mammoth, Old Faithful, along the Firehole River, in the Norris and Gibbon geyser basins, at Dragon's Mouth, and at Thumb on Yellowstone Lake.

The Water-That-Keeps-On-Coming-Out, as Shoshones called the geyser basins, must have held a special place among the spirits guiding Indian life, but no myths concerning thermal phenomena are known. Perhaps the nearest to a myth is a statement that roarings within the earth stemmed from the forging of weapons by infernal spirits, with each eruption the result of their terrible combat. Occasionally, according to one source, warriors would let water from a geyser spray onto their bodies to render them invisible when nearing an enemy.

MOUNTAIN MEN

The trappers and hunters known collectively as "mountain men" could almost be considered a latter-day tribe. They lived as close to the land as any of the Indians, they traveled widely, and they ultimately shaped the destiny of the northern plains and Rocky Mountains. Fur was their business—especially beaver—and as the slogan of the Hudson's Bay Company quipped, "For the pelts we collect, we risk our skins." It was literally true; the work was rugged in the extreme. A pouch of tobacco and a pipe were about the only items a mountain man allowed himself to carry, beyond clothes, a blanket, and traps. By the time of Lewis and Clark, French fur traders had already been in the plains for a century; after Lewis and Clark, the British and Americans entered in full force, riding horseback and pushing into virgin terrain inaccessible to *voyageurs'* canoes.

Osborne Russell, who trapped the Yellowstone country in the mid-1830s, recorded the details and the spirit of the era in his journal. He and a companion were wounded by Indians while they were camped along the shore of Yellowstone Lake, near the present Fishing Bridge. The companion—a greenhorn "who had been brot up in Missouri the pet of the family and had never done or learned much of anything but horseracing and gambling"—was lightly wounded but gravely panicked. Russell himself, seriously wounded, showed the resourcefulness typical of mountain men: "Well I said," he writes, "if you persist in thinking so you will die but I can crawl from this place upon my hands and one knee and Kill two or three Elk and make a shelter of the skins, and dry the meat until we get able to travel. . . ." And this he essentially did, caring for their wounds with "salt and water and . . . a salve of Beaver Oil and Castoreum."

Russell frequently noted Yellowstone's sights in his journal. One entry reads: ". . . we fell into a broken tract of country which seemed to be all on fire at some distance below the surface. . . . The treading of our horses sounded like traveling on a plank platform covering an immense cavity in the earth whilst the hot water and steam were spouting and hissing around us in all directions. As we were walking and leading our horses across this place the horse that was before me broke through the crust with one hindfoot and blue steam rushed from the hole. . . . Shortly after leaving this resemblance of the infernal regions we killed a fat buck Elk and camped at Sunset in a smooth grassy spot between two shaggy ridges watered by a small stream which came tumbling down the gorge behind us. . . .

"Some of the [geyser cones] are very serviceable to the hunter in preparing his dinner when hungry for here his kettle is always ready and boiling, his meat being suspended in the water by a string is soon prepared for his meal without further trouble. . . . Vast numbers of Black Tailed Deer are found in the vicinity of these springs and seem to be very familiar with hot waters and steam. The noise of which seems not to disturb their slumbers for

Bull elk

a Buck may be found carelessly sleeping where the noise will exceed that of three or four engines in operation."

Similar accounts came from the quills and lips of other mountain men who crossed Yellowstone pursuing the wealth of fur. The first of the lot— thirty years before Russell—was John Colter. He had pushed westward as a member of the Lewis and Clark expedition. Then in August 1806, as the party neared the Mandan Indian villages on the homeward journey, he re- quested permission to leave the company and spend the winter trapping along the headwaters of the Yellowstone River. This he did, working inde- pendently that first year and later joining the company headed by Manuel Lisa, a celebrated trader of the early days.

PUBLIC INTEREST

Colter brought stories of nature's spectacles out from his three years of sojourning in the wilderness. Some were held as fact and duly entered in the official expedition report written by Captain Clark in 1810. Others prompted skepticism, but the nation's editors set both the fanciful and the factual into type, and by Russell's time public curiosity had been whetted concerning this strange corner of "Louisiana," as the entire territory pur- chased from France was still called.

One report spawned another, with educated observers beginning to add their impressions to those of the frontiersmen. Warren Angus Ferris, a clerk with the American Fur Company, was one of the new, slightly more genteel breed entering Yellowstone. Recording his introduction to the Firehole area he commented: "I had heard in the summer of 1833, while at rendezvous [the annual trading and reveling assembly of the mountain men], that re- markable boiling springs had been discovered on the sources of the Madison by a party of trappers on their spring hunt; of which the accounts they gave were so very astonishing that I determined to examine them myself. . . ."

Ferris set out with two Indian companions, riding forty miles, "which was a hard day's ride, taking into consideration the rough irregularity of the country through which we traveled. . . . Immediately after supper [we] lay down to rest sleepy and much fatigued. The continual roaring of the springs, however . . . for some time prevented my going to sleep, and excited an impatient curiosity to examine them, which I was obliged to defer the gratifi- cation of until morning, and filled my slumbers with visions of waterspouts, cataracts, fountains, *jets d'eau* of immense dimensions, etc., etc.

"When I arose in the morning, clouds of vapor seemed like a dense fog to overhang the springs, from which frequent reports or explosions of differ- ent loudness constantly assailed our ears. . . . From the surface of a rocky plain or table, burst forth columns of water of various dimensions, project- ing high in the air, accompanied by loud explosions and sulphurous vapors. . . . After having witnessed three of them, I ventured near enough to put my hand into the waters of the basin, but withdrew it instantly, for the heat of the water in this immense caldron was altogether too great for my comfort; and the agitation of the water, the disagreeable effluvium continually exuding, and the hollow, unearthly rumbling under the rock on which I stood, so ill accorded with my notions of personal safety, that I retreated back precipitately to a respectful distance. The Indians, who were with me, were quite appalled and could not by any means be induced to approach them. They seemed astonished at my presumption in advancing up to the large one, and when I safely returned congratulated me upon my 'narrow escape.' "

By the 1830s the fur trade of the West was nearing its end. The decimation of the buffalo herds had begun, and beaver were already trapped close to elimination. Silk hats replaced beaver hats, hastening the destruction of the old fur market. During these last days Yellowstone was a crossroads for the men and the trade. The territories dominated by the three major fur companies—Hudson's Bay, Northwest Fur, and American Fur—converged in the Yellowstone region, and since the park area itself was hard to reach it was late to be exploited. There the fur era rang down its curtain, and in the process a new kind of interest was aroused. Colter, Russell, Ferris, Joe Meek, Daniel Potts, Jim Bridger—each man had stories to tell and knowledge to share. And increasingly the public wanted to listen.

Next to apply the growing knowledge of Yellowstone were prospectors seaching for gold. During the 1860s the Montana earth began to yield mineral wealth, and a floodtide of discovery swept across the mountains. In 1863 a party headed by Walter W. deLacy, an engineer, set out to prospect the high plateaus now encompassed by national park boundaries. Through all of August and into September the men followed the river courses and crossed the mountains and explored the geyser basins. But they found no ore, and deLacy did not bother even to publish his journal until much later. He did, however, publish a map, one of the first Yellowstone maps and quite accurate.

Other prospectors trailed through the park area, and claims and rude settlements began to dot the upper Yellowstone and Lamar rivers. A particular flurry centered at Gardiner. By 1870, America knew that the land of the Yellowstone held special beauties and curiosities, and the time had come for the next act in the long drama of man and wilderness: exploration for its own sake rather than for profit.

Yellowstone Lake

THE NATIONAL PARK

"Organized," proclaimed the *Montana Post* of 29 June 1867. "The expedition to the Yellowstone country mentioned a short time since is now organized, and . . . [will] start from the camp on Shield's River in about two weeks. . . . Parties who have the leisure to make this fascinating jaunt can ascertain particulars from Judge Hosmer or T. C. Everts."

But fate intervened. The territorial governor was accidentally drowned, and leading citizens expecting to explore Yellowstone were called to other matters. The few remaining went as far as Mud Volcano (in the vicinity of Yellowstone Falls) and then turned back without reporting much about what they had seen in that one short probe into the mysterious wilderness. The next two summers saw interest revived—and again thwarted, once before real plans had been laid, and once because an expected military escort could not be obtained.

Then three miners decided to go on their own, "believing that the dangers to be encountered had been magnified, and trusting by vigilance and good luck to avoid them. . . ."

INTO THE UPPER YELLOWSTONE

These three, each in his early thirties, worked together supplying water for placer mines at Diamond City, near Helena, Montana. Charles W. Cook, who had charge of the ditch company, was a New Englander who had moved west five years earlier. With him were David E. Folsom, a boyhood friend who had preceded Cook west, and William Peterson, a former Danish seaman who caught gold fever in San Francisco and had followed strikes from Idaho to British Columbia to Montana.

In September 1869 the three saddled up and, leading pack horses, started for the Gallatin Valley and entry into the headwater region of the Yellowstone River. "The long-talked-of expedition to the Yellowstone is off at last," the men's diary records, "but [stands] shorn of the prestige attached to the names of a score of the brightest luminaries in the social firmament of Montana, as it was first announced. It [now] has assumed proportions of utter insignificance, and of no importance to anybody in the world except the three actors themselves. . . . 'It is the next thing to suicide' . . . [was] the parting salutation that greeted our ears as we put spurs to our horses and left home and friends behind."

Charles W. Cook

At Bozeman the men tried to get others to join their party, but stirred no interest. Rumors of Yellowstone's wonders were widely known, but no one, not even Cook, Folsom, or Peterson, felt confident that anything truly remarkable lay beyond the barrier mountains. Even so, they laid in supplies for a six-week trip, including 175 pounds of flour, 30 pounds of sugar, 15 of coffee, 10 of salt, and a dozen boxes of yeast. There were also potatoes, bacon, a ham, "3 tin cups, 4 tin plates, 3 knives and forks, 3 spoons . . . 5 pairs of blankets, 2 buffalo robes," plus Colt pistols, ammunition, and fishing tackle.

Cook, elected captain by the other two, was assigned care of the field glasses "as a badge of his office," as Folsom recorded details of getting under way. Peterson, "having in former days been a sailor, is supercargo and general factotum, and carries two balls of stout cord for tying up specimens, taking soundings, etc. I once carried a surveyor's chain two days and am supposed to have a practical knowledge of topography, so I take charge of that department and cary a small pocket compass and thermometer."

For a month the three men explored the region of the present park, ascending the Yellowstone River to the lake, then crossing westward, and in time exiting via the Madison River. On return to Diamond City, Cook heard from an eastern friend who suggested an article detailing the trip and the discoveries, for the undertaking had proved of much wider interest and worth than the "three actors" had modestly predicted. Cook and Folsom combined their field diaries into a single account which Cook's friend, a writer named Clark, showed to editors at the *New York Tribune, Scribner's,* and *Harper's.* Each declined publication, explaining, as Clark passed the word back to Cook, that "they had a reputation that they could not risk with such unreliable material." In short, Yellowstone was too unusual to be believed. However, Clark did arrange publication in a lesser known Chicago periodical, the *Western Monthly Magazine.*

Cook and Folsom received eighteen dollars for their tale, which appeared in July 1879, ineptly cut by the magazine's editor. A few weeks later the issues of the magazine stored in a warehouse turned to ashes in the Chicago fire. Nevertheless, although the combination of bad editing and untimely flames kept the piece from receiving its full share of attention, key men read it, took note, and planned action. Random samples of the diary show why, for Folsom, Cook, and Peterson had gone about their work methodically and intelligently, savoring the experience and recognizing the special quality of the land they explored.

"*September 15.* [Cook] . . . had to sniff the vapor from every crevice and test the temperature of every spring; he barely missed paying for his rashness, for while descending a steep embankment from which the steam was rising in a hundred jets, one foot broke through the crust . . . of a crevice fifteen inches wide and several feet in depth; a headlong stumble, which ended in a roll in a bed of ashes saved him, for, on lowering the thermometer into the hole by string, the mercury instantly rose to 194°. . . . He took it very coolly and went on collecting specimens.

"*September 16.* As darkness approaches, the voice of the night breaks in upon the pervading stillness; the wolf scents us afar and the mournful cadence of his howl adds to our sense of solitude. The roar of the mountain lion awakens the sleeping echoes of the adjoining cliffs and we hear the elk whistling in every direction. . . .

David E. Folsom   *Mr. and Mrs. William Peterson*

"*September 20.* In some places [steam] spurted from the rocks in jets not larger than a pipe stem and in others it curled gracefully up from the surface of boiling pools from five to fifteen feet in diameter. In some springs the water was clear and transparent, others contained so much sulphur that they looked like pots of boiling yellow paint and one of the largest was as black as ink; near this was a fissure in the rocks . . . and we could hear the waters surging below, sending up a dull, resonant roar like the break of the ocean surf into a cave.

"*September 22.* We spent the day at the falls. . . . The ragged edge of the precipice tears the water into a thousand streams, changing it to the appearance of molten silver, all united together, yet separate. The outer ones decrease in size as they increase in velocity, curl outward and break into mist long before they reach the bottom.

"*September 23.* The cave [at Mud Volcano] seemed nearly filled with mud and the steam came with such force and volume that it would lift the whole mass against the roof and dash it out into the open space in front. . . . Our camp is half a mile away from it and yet we can distinctly hear every explosion. . . .

"*October 1.* . . . We concluded that the bottom had fallen out [after watching a preliminary surge and subsidence of Great Fountain Geyser], but the next instant, without any warning, it came rushing up and shot into the air at least eighty feet, causing us to stampede for higher ground.

"*October 2.* We followed up the Madison five miles, and there found the most gigantic hot springs we had seen. They were situated along the river bank, and discharged so much hot water that the river was warm a quarter of a mile below."

THE WASHBURN-LANGFORD-DOANE EXPEDITION

The men who had talked of going on the trip actually made by Cook, Folsom, and Peterson were fired with new enthusiasm by the 1869 reports, and the next summer a party set out. There were thirteen men led by the surveyor general of Montana Territory, Henry D. Washburn, and escorted by Lieutenant Gustavus C. Doane plus a sergeant and four privates. Folsom had gone to work for Washburn on return from his Yellowstone trip, so the new leader set forth armed with details of the Cook-Folsom-Peterson trip and also carrying a copy of a new map drawn the previous winter by deLacy. Still nobody quite dared to believe what they had heard and read. "I think a more confirmed set of skeptics never went out into the wilderness than those who composed our party," wrote one member of the expedition, Judge Cornelius Hedges, "and never was a party more completely surprised and captivated with the wonders of nature."

One discovery after another changed doubt into awed belief, from the canyon to the lake to the bubbling springs and mudpots. Nearing the end of the swing through the park, the expedition came upon Old Faithful. They chanced to edge out of the forest just as the geyser lifted its plume against the sunset sky, and in the next twenty-four hours they watched a dozen geysers play. Then on the night of 19 September 1870 they made a last camp before heading westward and out of the mountains. They spoke of the wonders they had seen and commented on the value of somehow protecting them in their natural state.

Folsom had recorded a similar thought nearly a year to the day before. "[This] is a scene of transcendent beauty which has been viewed by few white men," reads his last diary entry from along the shores of Yellowstone Lake, "and we felt glad to have looked upon it before its primeval solitude should be broken by the crowds of pleasure seekers which at no distant day will throng its shores." The 1870 party seconded this feeling.

Upon their return, members of the expedition spread the word of Yellowstone's worth, and since they were men of status they knew how to go about it both ambitiously and effectively. Hedges suggested in an article for the *Helena Herald* that Montana be extended to include the whole of Yellowstone, a suggestion at once chauvinistic and altruistic, for Congress might then be persuaded to deed title to the state as a park. Similar action had set aside Yosemite Valley a few years earlier; its lands had been withdrawn from settlement under federal law and entrusted to California for preservation.

Articles appeared also in *Scribner's* and the *Overland Monthly,* and Nathaniel P. Langford, Montana bank examiner and an ardent Yellowstone advocate, traveled east to gain the attention of influential men in Minneapolis, New York, and Washington. His efforts led to approval of an official exploration set for the following year, to be undertaken by the Geological Survey of the Territories.

Public interest in Yellowstone came from new tales of wildlife and exceptional geology, and perhaps even more from the poignant "Thirty-Seven Days of Peril" endured by Truman C. Everts, a member of the expedition who got lost while following the main party through the forest south of Yellowstone Lake. Everts had dismounted and returned to find his horse disappearing, carrying off all his gear. His colleagues searched for him in vain, cached food in the hope that he would find it, and went on, despairing. Everts himself, first in panic and then with resolution, set about making his way back to civilization, aided only by his pocket knife and a pair of opera glasses he was using as binoculars.

He experienced hallucinations, mistaking a lone white pelican swimming toward him for a canoe come to the rescue; he nearly burned to death when a fire built to keep away animals flared out of control during the night; and he scalded his hip by breaking through the crust of a steam vent he was sleeping beside for warmth. He felt hunger painfully accentuated by the lack of cooked food, and solved the problem by digging thistle roots and boiling them in hot springs. Later he improved his method of cooking by disassembling his opera glasses and using one of the lenses to focus the rays of the sun and start a fire.

Returning home, the main party sent out searchers who eventually found Everts, carried him to a trapper's cabin, gave him bear grease as medication and then food, and when he was strong enough helped him home from the wilderness. Writing of his experience, Everts concluded: ". . . I hope, under more auspicious circumstances, to revisit scenes fraught for me with such thrilling interest . . . to enjoy in happy contrast with the trials they recall, their power to delight, elevate, and overwhelm the mind with wondrous and majestic beauty."

THE HAYDEN SURVEY

Among the men in government approached by Langford on his trip east was Dr. Ferdinand V. Hayden, a geologist who agreed to conduct an official survey of Yellowstone the following summer if Congress voted the money. Fortunately, the appropriation was granted, and the expedition got under way on 15 July 1871, not long after snow had melted from the passes. This was by far the best staffed and equipped undertaking to date. It included two botanists, a zoologist, an entomologist, a mineralogist, a meteorologist, and a topographer, as well as geologist Hayden. There were also two artists and two photographers. Plants and animals were classified as the party rode along; geologic features were noted, sketched, and theorized upon; and maps were drawn, including one of Yellowstone Lake painstakingly made with the aid of a small, unsteady, canvas boat. Temperature readings were taken in more than six hundred hot springs. Landscape details were recorded with brush and camera, and place names were bestowed.

NATIONAL PARK

The reports and articles and speeches resulting from the Hayden expedition further swelled both public and political interest in safeguarding the region. In 1872 Congress passed a bill establishing Yellowstone as a national park, the first land in the world thought of and designated in just this way—land federally protected in its natural state for all time, for all people.

Expeditions now proliferated. As one early writer commented, Yellowstone became the most fully explored acreage of the West despite its complete lack of counties, townships, or villages. Travel remained rugged, yet each year brought increased visitors in a curious blend of official expeditions, sightseers, Indians, prospectors, and hunters bent on relating to the land in the old way. Sometimes paths and purposes crossed. For example, five years after the park's establishment, Chief Joseph led his band of Nez Perce warriors and families through Yellowstone as they neared the tragic end of their thirteen-hundred-mile flight toward Canadian sanctuary in preference to confinement on a reservation. Unfamiliar with the terrain, Joseph's men commandeered the services of two prospectors as guides, and near

Chief Joseph

Fountain Geyser they took two parties of tourists as hostages, eventually releasing them all.

It may be that such exciting evidence of a lingering frontier whetted public appetite for a "park adventure" even more than did the growing interest in scenic wonders. The numbers of visitors continued to grow, reaching into the ranks of the prestigious both at home and abroad. In 1883 President Chester Arthur arrived accompanied by a cabinet member, a senator, and other high civilian and military luminaries. They rode horseback, escorted by a full troop of cavalry and outfitted with a huge packstring and innumerable wranglers. Every twenty miles couriers were stationed to provide communication with the world beyond the mountains.

Ordinary citizens coped more personally and directly with travel. Two years before the President's visit, 150 miles of bridle path and 200 miles of road had been finished; however, as recorded in the park superintendent's annual report for 1881, visitor comment tended to be unfavorable. One man remarked that anyone who would permit women and children to travel such roads must be "an old scoundrel," and another claimed that the whole of the English language lacked adjectives to describe the discomfort of the main park road, "cut through heavy timber . . . the stumps left for two to twenty inches above ground."

Dust contributed additional misery, a problem inherently hard to solve. A turn-of-the-century superintendent, wanting money for road oil, looked forward to the visit of a congressman as a chance to win support for the project; but showers fell daily, settling the dust and ruining his hopes. On a similar occasion fate combined an absence of rain with abundant dust, and a congressional contingent deliberately placed last in a long procession of vehicles returned to Washington and voted funds to ease the park's road problem.

At first travel was by saddle horse, stagecoach, or wagon. From four to six horses pulled the coaches, which seated from six to thirty-three passengers. Trips typically lasted five days, sampling the park in a loop that held more beauty and experience than time let the mind absorb, according to one early traveler—John Muir—who commented, "Nothing can be done well at a pace of forty miles a day."

When automobiles began entering the park in 1915, the pace of travel quickened, although at first speed was limited to eight miles per hour when approaching a curve or passing another vehicle, ten when descending a steep grade, and twelve when ascending. In 1922 the limit was raised to a blanket twenty-five miles per hour, but with time limits set for travel between specified points: leave Gardiner on the north border of the park between 6:00 and 6:30 in the morning, and arrive at Norris between 8:30 and 9:00. Come rolling up ahead of schedule and you could be fined fifty cents a minute for the first five minutes and at twice that rate for the next twenty minutes. Be as early as twenty-five minutes, and you might either be fined twenty-five dollars or evicted from the park.

Roads and cars continue to be a problem even today. They have, however, opened the park beyond the "carriage trade" of the first decades, and they give a chance for individualized experience, in keeping with the spirit of direct involvement that engrossed the men who first saw Yellowstone and argued for it as a park.

The park idea—the concept of cherishing and preserving nature—had so many points of origin that a step-by-step chronology can hardly be traced. It is as if the idea were "right" and had found its time and place in mid-nineteenth-century Yellowstone. Wilderness had carried a largely negative meaning during the centuries of America's colonization and early development; it was untamed land to fear, to conquer, or in places simply wasteland to shun. Few persons attached particular value to the land for its own sake until romanticism began to stir in England, echoed on this continent by such writers as Whitman, Emerson, and Thoreau, and a contemporaneous school of painters. For the first time people began to see nature for itself, instead of for how it might be tailored to serve human purpose. Love of the wild fared especially well in the cities, with New York and San Francisco setting aside parks as green hearts for the urban streets and buildings soon to come.

On the frontier itself George Catlin, the renowned American painter, realized as early as 1832 that wildness was shrinking and that its loss would diminish the spirit of the nation. He urged the preservation of mid-continent land as a park where "man and beast" could continue forever to roam in primeval freedom. The French traveler de Tocqueville also commented on the role of wild land in America, bleakly finding the citizenry of the time "insensible to the wonders of nature, and they may be said not to perceive the mighty forests that surround them until [the trees] fall beneath the hatchet. Their eyes are fixed upon another sight. They . . . march across the wilds, draining swamps, turning the course of rivers, peopling solitudes, and subduing nature."

With the founding of Yellowstone National Park the nation demonstrated growing esthetic and scientific sensitivity. A national park was a new concept at the time, although some ninety nations now have parks patterned at least partly after Yellowstone—the first park of its kind ever, anywhere. More truthfully, the concept was new in the hearts of the mainstream society, for those who walked the continent before the arrival of European colonists had felt kinship with the whole of nature. Indians sensed belonging, not alienation. "One does not sell the earth upon which people walk," Chief Joseph had expressed it. "The earth was created by the assistance of the sun, and it should be left as it was. . . ."

Salsify

Natural History

Pilot Peak

GEOLOGY

The broad flats of Yellowstone—the "low" elevations—stand seven to eight thousand feet above sea level, and the Absaroka, Beartooth, and Gallatin mountain ranges bounding the park on the east, north, and west rise ten to eleven thousand feet. Volcanism shaped the general outlines of the landscape, and glaciation added its signature: fire and ice. The two together produce the hydrothermal features, volcanism supplying the heat, and glacial gravels permitting the percolation and storage of the water that bubbles and spurts from the earth.

VOLCANISM

The geologic lineage of Yellowstone reaches into the distant past, with Precambrian rocks on the Buffalo Plateau two-and-one-half billion to three billion years old, as ancient as any rocks known on the North American continent. However, geologically recent events are what distinguish the park and give it unique character. The oldest of these took place no more than fifty million years ago—"recent" on a scale that begins time with the origin of the planet itself about five billion years ago.

During the Eocene Epoch lavas poured from the earth throughout the Rocky Mountain region, and explosions mixed hot ash with mud and fragments of existing rock, forming breccia. Ridges and peaks in the Beartooth and Absaroka ranges today date from these eruptions and breccia flows. So does Specimen Ridge in Lamar Valley, formed as gigantic mudflows swept from unstable slopes high in the Absarokas and inched across outlying country, overriding and burying everything in their wake. Forests were inundated and fossilized layer on layer, as life was repeatedly buried, regained its claim, and was again buried. Similar petrified forests dating from the same general time as those of Specimen Ridge are found in the Gallatin Mountains.

For five or ten million years the Eocene activity continued. Then came quiet and a long period of erosion; and, after it, another fiery round of volcanism. This new episode ranks among the outstanding spectacles of the continent's recent geologic history. Earth changes are seldom abrupt or massive, but during a period that may have lasted only a few days the Yellowstone earth spewed out enough volcanic debris to devastate the entire park area. Ashflows raced at speeds probably greater than one hundred miles per hour, veneering every contour and extinguishing all life in their paths. Canyons and valleys that had eroded into the old volcanic landscape were filled by the new volcanic outpouring. Vents shot out gas mixed with hot ash and fragments of barely solidified rhyolite, raining debris over the countryside for hundreds of miles. In the area of the vents themselves sheets of hot pumice, ash, and rock particles blanketed the land, welding themselves together with their own internal heat and sheer weight. Some of these deposits, called welded tuff, are over one thousand feet thick. They are found throughout the park, perhaps most readily recognizable at Mount Everts and Golden Gate, near Mammoth, and at Norris.

As the magma welled out, the rock roof of the rapidly emptying chamber lost support and collapsed, in the same way that Mount Mazama, Oregon, gutted itself and collapsed inward to produce Crater Lake. Crater Lake's majestic five-mile diameter is dwarfed, however, by the comparative magnitude of the Yellowstone caldera, as such "craters" are properly termed. Only traces of the gigantic Yellowstone caldera remain. Parts of its walls have been identified near Norris on the Madison Plateau, and near Mount Sheridan and the Flat Mountain Arm of Yellowstone Lake. The diameter varies from thirty to forty-five miles, and the depth was probably five or six thousand feet at the time of the collapse, a chasm almost beyond imagining—yet ephemeral. Magma had risen, burst the earth's surface, and caused the great collapse; then it rose again, this time simply pushing up the floor of the entire caldera and changing it from a depression to a slightly rounded dome, its center just east of Old Faithful. Most of today's thermal basins in the western portion of the park and at West Thumb along the lake shore are in rocks that mark the outer rim of the old caldera.

The first mammoth Yellowstone caldera formed about 750,000 years ago, and perhaps 150,000 years later a similar chain of events led to another, smaller caldera. Walls of this second chasm are still partially distinguishable in the Mount Washburn area and at Lake Butte, indicating a diameter of about twenty miles. Its floor, too, was pushed up into a dome, with its center in the area between today's canyon and the lake.

Fractures around the edges of both calderas issued a succession of flows, filling and overflowing depressions and leaving great plateaus and cliffs. The composition of the molten material was rhyolite, the same as that of the earlier, violent ashflows, but this time the form was different. These new outpourings were a viscous, slow-moving fluid. Where the ashflow tuffs were built up from a rapid series of pulsations and cooled as single units, the new flows welled out slowly in a single mass, forming tongues with towering, fairly sheer lead edges. A drillhole recently bored in the Nez Perce flow penetrated seven hundred feet without cutting through any interfaces and without reaching through more than an estimated two-thirds of the original thickness of the rhyolite. Firehole Canyon cuts between two of these rhyolite flows, one that came from the east, the other from the southwest.

GLACIATION

The most recent of the rhyolite flows took place about 70,000 years ago, as indicated by potassium argon dating. Some magma probably welled up under thick caps of ice, or flowed against ice, causing a sudden chilling and shattering, for by that time glaciers were advancing over the Yellowstone country. The shattered rhyolite formed a glassy sand which was carried along by the moving ice and by streams of meltwater. The shiny black particles conspicuous in Black Sand Basin furnish an example easily seen today.

Ice ages have repeatedly gripped the North American continent, the first one possibly dating back two-and-one-half million years, and the most recent (the Wisconsin Ice Age) lasting from roughly 120,000 to 12,000 years ago. In Yellowstone, ice of Wisconsin age twice shielded all but the highest peaks. It began by creeping down from the heights of the Absarokas; then the ice thickened to about four thousand feet, so immense an amount that individual glaciers coalesced and eventually reversed their direction of flow. Instead of inching westward down the mountain valleys as separate tongues, ice capped the entire Yellowstone uplands and turned back on itself to override the crest of the Absaroka Range. It molded promontories with their more gentle, leeward slopes oriented to the east, and it rounded the headwalls of cirques that had been cut earlier by the westward-flowing alpine glaciers. Boulders of rhyolite tuff were even carried from the lower, western slopes of the mountains over the crest of the range to the east, where they lie today as classic glacial erratics. Other erratics, easily seen from present roads, dot the Lamar Valley, and an enormous erratic boulder lies beside the road in the thick lodgepole pine forest near the rim of the Yellowstone canyon.

Glacial erratic

At its maximum, the second of the great icecaps in the park mantled nearly four thousand square miles, an immense area reaching not only over the Absarokas but also down the Snake River drainage to merge into the piedmont glacier at the base of the Teton Mountains. The ice plucked and ground hard rock into fragments; it directly bulldozed loose gravels; and its meltwater further churned and transported gravels, sands, and silts. When the forward thrust of the glacier finally ended, the reworking of the land surface went on. Disintegrating ice dropped its accumulated loads of debris, and meltwater loaded with sediments banked gravel and sand against the changing ice, further shaping the landscape.

Yellowstone Lake dates from this time, its immense size formed directly from the melt of wasting ice and as runoff from the land impounded against the ice. Water flowed around the edge of an enormous melting block, in time ringing it except along the western side where the ice seems to have remained in contact with the edge of the Central Plateau. Terraces from these early water levels as high as three hundred feet above the present level of the lake are clearly seen today in Hayden Valley and above the lake. Outflow from the lake drained northward and added its sculpturing force to the cutting of the Grand Canyon of the Yellowstone, which had been formed earlier by overflow from a lake filling the second caldera.

Yellowstone River

Blacktail Plateau in winter

By about 12,500 years ago the stagnant ice had released most of the land; plants had returned, mammals were again grazing the Yellowstone plateaus, and man either had already come with his spears and atlatls or would soon arrive. The ice age had completed its chapter—or so everyone supposed. Then in 1931 a road crew working near Tower Junction cut against the northern toe of a cliff—and exposed clear, glassy, blue-gray ice, running horizontally for at least six hundred feet and apparently free of embedded debris. About two feet of rock rubble had overlain it, shielding it. The thickness of the ice was not determined, for the business at hand was to build the road from Mammoth to Tower rather than to delay for investigation of the ice mass. An insulating fill of gravel was simply laid over the ice, and asphalting continued.

The best guess is that this ice body is a remnant from the ice age. It could scarcely have formed under the climatic conditions since that time, certainly not so clear and clean and hard as this ice is reported to have been. If this is correct, it can truly be said that the ice age still affects Yellowstone, for the roadway 5.15 miles west of Tower Junction keeps sinking and needing repair as this finger of the Pleistocene reaches into the automobile age.

THERMAL FEATURES

The great furnace of magma that caused Yellowstone's volcanic flows and eruptions still fires the landscape. The best estimates indicate a body of magma around 1700°F. lying ten thousand feet or more beneath Yellowstone's surface and measuring about twenty-eight miles wide by forty miles long. Heat for the park's geysers and hot springs and mudpots comes from this magma. Water comes mostly from rainstorms and snow melt—especially snow. The melt and runoff seep into the ground through pores and cracks and collect in porous subterranean layers formed of rock rubble deposited as glacial outwash and gravel dropped in lakes that ponded against remnant ice masses. Such beds lie two hundred feet thick within the geyser basins, capable of holding an enormous quantity of water. An additional small source of water, equaling perhaps 5 percent of the total, comes from "juvenile water" condensing for the first time from hydrogen and oxygen present in the magma.

To the heat and the water reservoirs, add one more ingredient necessary for geysers: a lid. Minerals dissolved deep underground by hot water are precipitated near the surface as the water rises and cools. Layers of sediment close to the surface become impregnated and cemented into locally hard beds while, on the surface, minerals are deposited as geyserite or sinter, the gleaming white rock that caps large portions of many thermal basins. The hard layers of both the cemented sediments and the sinter act as a lid for the underground circulation systems, causing temperatures and pressures to mount high enough for eruptions.

With little exception, weather and season have no effect on eruptions or hot springs because the sources of heat and water underlying thermal basins are too vast. Water circulates slowly but freely through interconnected spaces and cracks within the ground. It is heated by conduction from the magma, acting through intervening layers. The scale of the underground system is simply too enormous to be affected by short-range events above ground. At most, wind, barometric pressure, and air temperature can alter only details of an eruption, such as the exact timing or the appearance of the water and steam plume shooting from the vent.

Perhaps ten thousand geysers, hot springs, and steam vents break the surface of the land within park boundaries, most of them beyond reach of roads and only about five hundred of them named. The total heat given off could theoretically melt more than fourteen tons of ice each second, or over a million tons per day—the equivalent of ice one foot thick and one hundred feet wide stretching nearly ten miles. Water temperatures near the surface vary from one feature to the next, from less than 100° up to 213°F., with each individual geyser or spring holding its own temperature fairly steadily. Measuring deep temperatures poses several problems, in part because the inner "pipes" of thermal features are not smooth-bore conduits, but a series of irregular cavities and cracks, frequent angles, and constrictions, and are constantly subject to clogging as minerals are precipitated from the hot water. Lowering an instrument into such a system gives data valid only for conditions near the surface. Old Faithful has been probed for nearly six hundred feet, but with no way of knowing how much of this represented vertical depth. A temperature of 284°F. was recorded, with repeated short-term surges of a few degrees owing to the convection circulation of water within the geyser system. A borehole in the Norris Basin was drilled to 1,088 feet, revealing a temperature of 460°F. Similar research holes in Yellowstone and other thermal areas of the world suggest that, in order for natural geysers to exist, water temperatures deep within the ground must be at least 300° F. (and they are known to be as high as 600°F.). Below this range, heat dissipates in other ways. Rising temperatures lessen the viscosity of water and increase its rate of circulation; this is significant in view of the extremely small openings of geyser feeder tubes. Heat also increases the solvent action of water, permitting it to dissolve silica and other minerals deep underground and thus enlarge openings as it flows.

Four general types of thermal features characterize Yellowstone: geysers, hot springs, mudpots, and fumaroles. To the eye they differ considerably, but actually each is a different expression of the same basic phenomenon, a different system of releasing heat from the same deep-earth source, depending on local balances of heat, water, and mud from decomposed rock.

A fumarole is a vent that gives off only steam and other gases; it is a dry system.

A mudpot has essentially the same inner structure as a fumarole, but near the surface it has a bowllike depression in which rain and snow collect and steam condenses to liquid water. Hot gases escaping from the magma add to the furor—and smell. Those often present include carbon dioxide (odorless), hydrogen sulphide (smelling like rotten eggs), and sulphur dioxide (producing a sharp, choking feeling). The sulphur gases form sul-

Mudpot

phuric acid, which reacts with rock to form the mud that bubbles and plops like simmering stew as steam rises through it.

A hot spring has inner plumbing that lets hot water rise fairly freely to the surface. The heat dissipates steadily, and consequently the spring maintains equilibrium.

Geysers are distinguished from hot springs by eruptions, whether spurts only a foot high or towering plumes of one hundred feet or more. (Old Faithful's jets average about 130 feet, and Steamboat Geyser in Norris Basin, presently the largest geyser in the world, shoots 300 feet.) Eruptions may be sporadic or regular, as frequent as every minute or as infrequent as every few hours or days, or even years. Most geysers erupt irregularly. Even Old Faithful varies from known extremes of 33 to 96 minutes between eruptions, although its "faithful" average based on 46,214 recorded observations is 64.91 minutes. The inner workings of all geysers are delicately balanced, depending on particular sets of critical temperatures, volumes of water, and timing. All are easily upset, and all are certain to change as subterranean conditions change. The Hebgen earthquake of 1959, with its epicenter only thirty miles from park geyser systems, caused widespread change, both temporary and long range. Dozens of hot springs that had not previously erupted spouted water at least briefly after the earthquake, and a few geysers that had been active for years dropped into sudden dormancy. Temperatures changed, some up, some down; and water that had been clear, clouded. Many changes were immediate; others showed up weeks or years after the quake. Some lasted only briefly; others have continued.

GEYSER ERUPTIONS

In general, geysers can be said to erupt as a result of the deep circulation of water heated to high temperatures. Pressure within the earth causes water to boil at higher temperatures than on the surface, somewhat as barometric pressure affects the boiling point on the surface of the earth ($212°$F. at sea level and around $198°$F. in Yellowstone, depending on exact elevation). The greater the depth within the earth, the greater the pressure; and the greater the pressure, the higher the temperature needed for boiling. Consequently, hundreds of feet within the earth even "superheated" water is not boiling. However, it does rise; it is lighter than cool water, weighing only about three quarters as much at $600°$F. as at freezing. As the heated water rises, the pressure on it decreases. When the pressure has decreased enough, boiling begins.

The first few bubbles can rise freely. Then they start to become numerous and expand faster than constrictions to the geyser plumbing will let them rise. Their upward rush begins to act almost like an inverted plunger, forcing water upward in the main geyser tube. A preliminary overflow or a series of tentative spurts reduces pressure near the top of the water column. Water at depth suddenly bursts into steam, its volume explosively increasing hundreds of times. This releases more pressure. More water changes into steam, and the full eruption is on.

How long it lasts depends on how much water the individual geyser has available in its local plumbing system, plus water temperature and how fast it spurts out. When the supply of water gives out, the eruption stops. Feeder cracks and channels keep steady trickles flowing into the geyser system, replenishing reservoirs, and eventually enough water and enough heat are regained for a new eruption. The length of the recovery period varies from geyser to geyser and time to time, although prediction is possible within a few minutes for a few geysers, some of which are even more reliably predictable than Old Faithful.

WORLD THERMAL AREAS

Oddities in nature often diminish into mere sideshows as human familiarity lessens awe. Yet the thermal activity of Yellowstone is exceedingly rare and highly valuable both esthetically and scientifically. Hot springs are known in many parts of the world, particularly around the Pacific Rim where ancient volcanic rifts still give off heat, but geysers are rare. Only Chile, Kamchatka '(a peninsula off Siberia), New Zealand, Iceland, and Yellowstone have significant geysers—with more in Yellowstone than anywhere else.

In California an area called The Geysers is a misnomer; it is a region of deep thermal activity that is being tapped as a power source, but there are no true geysers and never have been. A scattered few places in other western states do have true geysers, the largest and naturally most beautiful belonging to the Beowawe area of north central Nevada. These have been destroyed, however, in the search for geothermal power. Pipes and valves now cap them; gases escape, hissing and roaring, and minerals precipitate on the iron, sealing over every square inch of metal with sinter. Similarly, the power of most of Iceland's and New Zealand's geysers today fires industry, rather than imagination.

In Yellowstone the opposite choice has been made. The thermal basins remain part of nature's pattern. White plumes of water and steam still lift against the sky. Water ouzels and Wilson's snipes feed along the margins of hot-water streams, warming themselves by steam vents, in winter, and then stalking after insects. In Norris Geyser Basin, a sagebrush lizard (*Sceloporous graciosus graciosus*) seems to be a holdover from long ago when the climate was much warmer; hot ground enables the species to continue living there. At Mammoth and in the Ragged Hills at Norris, coyotes and bears den where ground temperatures are 30°F. warmer inside their caves than outside, and air temperatures are 10°F. warmer. Life and land continue their own timeless course. Yellowstone geology seems extraordinary to the mind of modern man, but is normal for species native to the area. Its resources are to be utilized or avoided, depending on circumstance.

PLANTS

Yellowstone plants vary according to elevation and soil conditions: white-bark pine at timberline, with more than 150 annual rings to an inch of growth; sagebrush and rabbitbrush on the lowland flats along the park's north boundary; meadows of grass and sedge and flowers. Such variety is readily noticed and understood. It results directly from growing conditions. Other types of variety, and of change within various plant communities of the park, are only beginning to be understood.

THE ROLE OF FIRE

An example is the way fire serves as midwife for lodgepole pine, which makes up the main type of forest in the park. The small, prickly cones of these pines open less than halfway under usual conditions. Enough seeds fall to perpetuate the species, but a reserve stays within the cones, sealed by resin. For ten or twenty years, or even eighty years, the seeds may be imprisoned, yet still capable of germinating when released. Cones may grow firmly into the trunk of a tree, yet keep their seeds viable, and cones cached and forgotten by squirrels hold their potential of life safely locked within by the resin, waiting.

Fire commonly acts as the releaser. Its heat melts the cone resin and breaks the seal. It also cleanses the soil of competing plants, including the parent trees, and given this fresh start as many as three hundred thousand seedling pines per acre may spring up. If even a fraction establish themselves, the resulting forest will stand dense and spindly. Trees a century old and fully mature will measure only three or four inches in diameter—long poles, self-pruned of branches except for a burst of green foliage at their high tops. Or, if seedlings are wide spaced and competition for light is not keen, these same trees will be a foot in diameter and stoutly branched throughout.

Historically, fire has reset the cycle of the entire Yellowstone forest community, not just of individual trees or even species, for the fresh shoots that emerge phoenixlike from the ashes forge an entire new chain of life. Mice and rabbits feed on the tender sprouts, and in turn their flesh becomes food for owls and weasels and coyotes. Deer and moose benefit from increased shrubby browse, and when the new pines at last produce cones, birds such

Harebell

as crossbills and siskins arrive to feast on seeds, and woodpeckers come to chisel after beetles and grubs.

Flames may sweep the lodgepole forest anew, devouring the needles that blanket its floor, scorching the trees, and freeing seeds locked within the accumulating cones. Or, without fire, the increasing shade of the forest may be suitable in some areas for Engelmann spruce and subalpine fir to germinate, and the nature of the forest will slowly shift away from pine. Eventually, lightning will strike, and fire will rewind nature's clock and set the pattern of life in motion again—or at least this is the usual cycle. In Yellowstone, however, a variation has been noticed. Unlike lodgepole cones elsewhere, cones in the park rarely delay their opening, but tend to open as soon as they mature, dispersing their seeds immediately without hoarding a portion for release later by fire.

Why this happens nobody can really say, although speculation suggests that the need for delayed opening may have lessened. This hypothesis holds that lodgepoles probably pioneered Yellowstone plateaus as handmaidens of wildfire, gaining dominance so successfully that spruce and fir were essentially eliminated from competition. As the towering spires of these species became fewer, lightning no longer set the forest ablaze every few years, for trees tall enough to punctuate the overall canopy of a forest are known to act as lightning rods, channeling the fury of thunderclouds from sky to earth. With fire reduced, lodgepoles no longer needed a reserve of cones held for later opening by flames, and they began instead to cast their seed immediately, speeding all possible progeny toward superabundant new green life. But a few decades of observing are not enough to reveal the whole story—and partial truth can too easily masquerade as full truth.

An example of too simple an explanation for a complex situation is the previously assumed relationship between elk and aspen. Groves of aspen trees fringe the grasslands of Yellowstone between Mammoth and Tower and on into Lamar Valley. The summer wind dance of their shining green leaves contrasts with the somber tones of the conifer forest, and in autumn their gold adds glory to drives such as the back road that circles Bunsen Peak, or the one crossing the uplands from Blacktail Pond to Tower Junction. The beauty of aspen is renowned, yet those in the park have seemed threatened. They are tasty. Elk hungry for winter browse strip bark from aspen as high as they can reach and nip off twigs and new shoots that might otherwise perpetuate the groves by vegetative reproduction.

A large population of elk wintering in the northern park and a simultaneous decline of aspen seemed to point toward indictment of the foraging herds. Furthermore, the loss of the trees apparently also fostered the loss of certain animal species. Whitetail deer disappeared from the park in the 1930s, supposedly forced out by the elk because of competition for winter browse. New evidence, however, indicates that whitetail deer may never have wintered inside the park and that their disappearance from the area is owing to changes outside of Yellowstone's boundary, not inside. About the same time the loss of the deer was noticed—for whatever reason—beaver began to decline in the Tower Falls area. Photographs taken there in the early 1920s show aspen stumps cut by beaver, but bushy with new growth pushing up from the roots. Under usual circumstances such natural coppicing is sufficient for aspen to replenish itself and allow beaver to return even after eating themselves part way out of a food supply and forcing a temporary shift in territory; but by the thirties, aspen and beaver both seemed to be going from the Tower Falls area. Elk seemed to have caused the loss.

Now, however, other factors are believed to have triggered the change. Prolonged drought had weakened the aspen, and a simultaneous lessening of wildfire furthered their decline since aspen, like lodgepole pine, is a species generally dependent on periodic flame for replenishment. In the past, fires maintained enough vigorous aspen stands to withstand extensive foraging, but today that cycle has been interrupted. In the comparative moment that Yellowstone has been a national park—one century—man has worked valiantly to check the force of fire, a concept now questioned as unwise in many situations. Black devastation follows flame as an immediate, obvious effect; but the full role of fire reaches much further and affects relationships only beginning to be recognized.

PETRIFIED FORESTS

Scattered ridges and peaks across the northern park hold petrified forests stacked in layers one on top of another like a gigantic cake. This is the only

Petrified trees

place in the world where successive forests have been preserved in stone. A lone sample of a petrified tree stands close to the road near Tower Junction, accessible by car, and more spectacular examples lie in remote canyons of the Gallatin Range and stud the ledges of Specimen Ridge, which bounds Lamar Valley on the south. At least twenty-seven successive forests stand in their original locations, and one estimate places the number at forty-four separate forests. Trunks still stand upright—tall stumps ten to fifteen feet high and as much as four feet in diameter. Leaves and needles and cones fallen from the trees are perfectly preserved as fossils. More than one hundred forest species are present, including ferns, shrubs, and such trees as sycamore, walnut, magnolia, redwood, and a relative of Asia's breadfruit tree.

Other, better known fossil forests such as Petrified Forest National Park in Arizona, or the Gingko Forest of Washington and the Calistoga Forest of California, preserve trees that were carried like driftwood by ancient streams, then buried by sediments. In Yellowstone, the trees were petrified where they stood. Repeated volcanic outbursts spewed smothering clouds of ash and blobs of glowing lava. Debris rode the superheated clouds of gas and rained to earth, killing plants directly and driving animals ahead of its deadly swath. Immense loose deposits piled deep and began to inch forward as avalanches and mudflows, slowly engulfing trees without toppling them.

Periods of dormancy interspersed with eruptions. Plants pioneered the rich volcanic outfall. Soil formed, and forests again flourished. Then huge fissures burst into renewed activity. Layer on layer, chapter by alternate chapter, the record built itself. Specimen Ridge, perhaps the most spectacular example in the park, rises twelve hundred feet above Lamar Valley. In time, it represents a tick of the geologic clock which lasted about twenty thousand years during the Eocene Epoch, forty or fifty million years ago.

HOT GROUND

Plants roughly indicate temperature changes in the ground surrounding Yellowstone's hot springs and geysers. Where heat is intense, soil becomes bare. If thermal activity diminishes and the ground temperature lowers, lodgepole pine quickly invades. Trees of varying heights mark the progressive cooling of the soil: saplings where the cooling began, seedlings closer to the remaining heat. In the opposite situation, with hot earth expanding from a meadow toward a forest, the first sign of a rising ground temperature may be a patch of dying grass. A few years later successive rings of dead and dying pines will mark the spreading heat. Closest will be a scattering of fallen trees; next, defoliated snags still standing, and, behind them, pines turning the telltale reddish brown of impending death. When encroaching heat first affects lodgepoles they often bear extra heavy cone crops. Doom awaits the individual trees, but, as they die, excess seed production guarantees a future for the species.

Hot ground also affects small plants. A thermal grass, *Panicum thermali,* thrives at soil temperatures up to 104°F. and in fact depends on the heat for survival. In winter it forms tight rosettes of overlapping blades so wide and closely whorled that the plant looks more like an herb than a grass. In this compact form it hugs the warm world within an inch or two of the ground and completely avoids the subzero reality of Yellowstone's winter.

Monkeyflower, too, flourishes through the winter in rosette form, growing at the edge of steamy, snow-free vents and along the banks of hot-spring overflows. When April and May bring warmth back to the air, this species stretches forth longer stems and opens yellow blossoms a month or two ahead of most other Yellowstone flowers.

HOT WATER

Bacteria, a single-cell form of plant life, thrive in hot springs at temperatures up to 204°F. where they grow as delicate filaments encased in gelatinous sheaths. Algae also live in Yellowstone's hot water although only up to about 167°F. This upper limit is apparently set by a breakdown of the photosynthesizing mechanism; protoplasm itself could endure higher temperatures.

Both algae and bacteria are distributed according to water temperature, with the amount of light available also playing a role. Green and blue pigments intensify when light levels are low, even responding when clouds screen the sun. On the other hand, yellow and orange pigments lack this sensitivity to changes and tolerate a greater amount of light. Wherever algae are at the upper limit of their temperature range and their growth is thin and patchy, the colors will be varying yellows and oranges. However, where temperatures are optimum and mats of algae have grown thick, green and blue pigments will build up beneath the protection of surface cells. At the very bottom of such mats, the light may be too meager for algae to thrive but ideal for bacteria, and the foundations of these mats will be filaments of bacteria.

A considerable life chain develops from the primitive plants of the park's hot springs. Brine flies and their larvae eat the algae, several species restricting their entire lives to a vertical habitat of water plus the air immediately above it. As larvae they live in the water, and as adults they feed over it and also walk about submerged in bubbles of air which keep them dry and act as a heat shield. Living on the brine flies are other, parasitic species of flies and also an aquatic red mite. The flies and mites, in turn, are preyed upon by spiders and carabid beetles stalking the edges of runoff channels, ready to dash onto the algae mats to capture prospective meals, then scamper back to dry ground to feast. Dragonflies also hunt at the hot springs, preying on flies, mites, and spiders—but not on beetles, which are too hard. Birds feed both on the life forms directly associated with the springs and on those that have inadvertently fallen victim to the heat of the water or the ground.

TREES AND FLOWERS TO WATCH FOR

About three-fourths of the park is clothed with lodgepole pine, monotonous in its dense stands cloaking the high interior plateaus. Yet these forests have beauty—a strong geometric pattern formed by the upright lines of their trunks interwoven with shafts of light and shadow. When snow blankets the forest, any time from September to July, the pattern takes on a special boldness with vertical black trunks and horizontal black shadows set squarely on a field of white.

Limber pine occurs at Mammoth and at other low elevations of the park. Its needles, five to the bundle, are long and give the twigs a feather-duster appearance. Whitebark pine, like limber pine, belongs to the higher elevations of the park, ranging to timberline at about ten thousand feet. It is most easily seen on Mount Washburn, often growing contorted by wind and the blasting of snow. Groves of subalpine fir intermix with the whitebark pine and reach down as low as seventy-five hundred feet.

The road into Yellowstone from the south passes through forests of Engelmann spruce and subalpine fir, taller and more massive trees than the lodgepole. Near Mammoth and along the road to Tower, Douglas fir predominates. All three species bear needles singly rather than in bunches, as is true of pines. Spruce needles are sharper pointed than those of subalpine fir or Douglas fir and tend to be four-sided instead of flat.

The flower calendar of the park begins in May with buttercup, phlox, and pasqueflower showing modestly among clumps of sagebrush. Later bitterroot adds its brilliant, ground-hugging pink, and wild geraniums, scarlet gilia, and blue flax wave from slender stalks. By early July clumps of balsamroot color hillsides yellow with their sunflowerlike blossoms, and lupine adds rich shades of purple. Everts thistle pushes up coarse stalks three feet high in meadows and along stream banks, and green gentian forms remarkable spikes as much as five feet high on moist slopes at the edge of forests.

Dunraven Pass, on Mount Washburn, is the most easily accessible alpine meadow in the park. Slopes become gardens as soon as winter's snow releases its grip. Paintbrush, larkspur, harebell, bluebell, columbine, yarrow, fireweed, cow parsnip, mountain hollyhock—species after species, color after color, flowers paint the slopes.

RED AND PINK FLOWERS

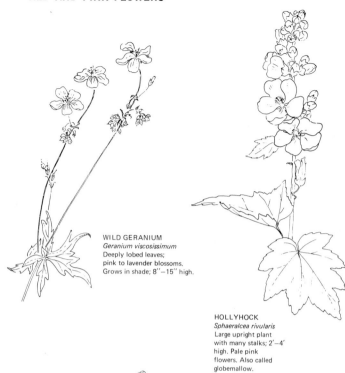

WILD GERANIUM
Geranium viscosissimum
Deeply lobed leaves;
pink to lavender blossoms.
Grows in shade; 8''–15'' high.

HOLLYHOCK
Sphaeralcea rivularis
Large upright plant
with many stalks; 2'–4'
high. Pale pink
flowers. Also called
globemallow.

SCARLET GILIA
Gilia aggregata
Brilliant red flowers,
conspicuous in
Jackson Hole and now
invading northward
into Yellowstone.
About 12'' high.

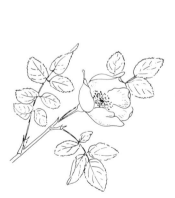

BITTERROOT
Lewisia rediviva
Intense pink blossom
pushing directly up
from the earth
without noticeable
stem or leaves;
2''–3'' in diameter.

INDIAN PAINTBRUSH
Castilleja
Many species. Flowers
vary from scarlet to
orange. Typically
8''–12'' high.

WILDROSE
Rosa
Pink flowers and red fruits; prickly
bushes. Four similar species in
the park, all looking like garden roses
except small and single.

PRAIRIE SMOKE
Sieversia ciliata
Hairy leaves, dusky pink-purple petals,
feathery seedheads; 6''–10'' high.

PURPLE AND BLUE FLOWERS

FRINGED GENTIAN
Gentiana thermalis
Deep blue petals with
delicately fringed edges;
5''–8'' tall.

LUPINE
Lupinus
Spikes of showy blue and purple
flowers; a dozen species in the
park from 4'' or 5'' to over a
foot high.

HAREBELL
Campanula rotundifolia
Deep blue,
flowers often
nodding;
5''–10'' tall.
Slender stalks.

WILD FLAX
Linum lewisii
About a foot high. Pale
blue flowers
floating on delicate
stems.

BEARDSTONGUE PENSTEMON
Penstemon
Tubular flowers with
blue to purple petals,
touched with pink in
some species; 15 species
in the park, from 8'' to
over 2' high.

LARKSPUR
Delphinium bicolor
Showy blue. Blooms in
thermal areas, 10''–12'' high.
Other species to 3' high.

YELLOW AND WHITE FLOWERS

MONKEYFLOWER
Mimulus
Bright yellow
tubular flower
with long lower
lip; about 5 species
in the park,
including a dwarf
mimulus that grows
close to hot springs.

YARROW
Achillea lanulosa
Flat heads with
myriad tiny white
flowerlets;
feathery leaves.
1'—2' high.

GREEN GENTIAN
Frasera speciosa
Tall, coarse stalks 2'—5' high;
flowers greenish-white with
soft purple dots.

STONECROP
Sedum stenopetalatum
Grows close to the ground with
succulent stems and leaves,
yellow flowers. Frequent on
thermal ground.

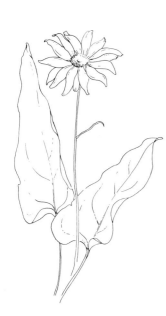

BALSAMROOT
Balsamorhiza sagittata
Blooms early. Large yellow
sunflowerlike blossoms;
numerous upright leaves.
About a foot high.

BUSH CINQUEFOIL
Potentilla fruticosa
Sturdy shrub 2'—3' high
with gray-green foliage and
small lemon-yellow flowers.

ARNICA
Arnica cordifolia
Brilliant yellow
flowers 2'' across
on stems 12''—15'' high;
10 species in the park.

TREES AND BUSHES

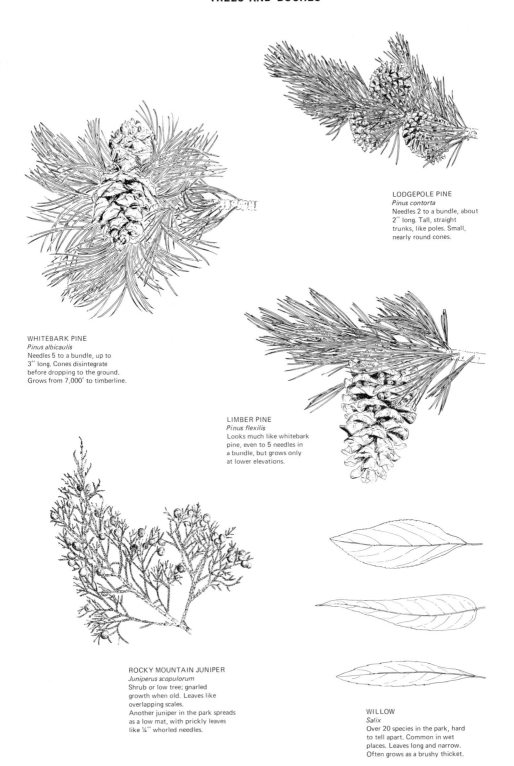

LODGEPOLE PINE
Pinus contorta
Needles 2 to a bundle, about
2'' long. Tall, straight
trunks, like poles. Small,
nearly round cones.

WHITEBARK PINE
Pinus albicaulis
Needles 5 to a bundle, up to
3'' long. Cones disintegrate
before dropping to the ground.
Grows from 7,000' to timberline.

LIMBER PINE
Pinus flexilis
Looks much like whitebark
pine, even to 5 needles in
a bundle, but grows only
at lower elevations.

ROCKY MOUNTAIN JUNIPER
Juniperus scopulorum
Shrub or low tree; gnarled
growth when old. Leaves like
overlapping scales.
Another juniper in the park spreads
as a low mat, with prickly leaves
like ¼'' whorled needles.

WILLOW
Salix
Over 20 species in the park, hard
to tell apart. Common in wet
places. Leaves long and narrow.
Often grows as a brushy thicket.

TREES AND BUSHES

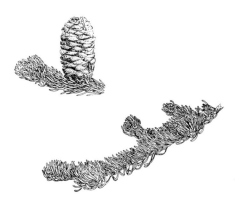

DOUGLAS FIR
Pseudotsuga menziesii
Needles soft to the touch. Cones
about 3″ long with conspicuous
lobed "tongue" on outside of
each scale.

SUBALPINE FIR
Abies lasiocarpa
Also called balsam fir. Needles stiff
and brushed upward except on branch
tips with cones, where they mat the
entire stem evenly. Cones stand
upright; disintegrate on the tree.
Grows at high elevations.

ENGELMANN SPRUCE
Picea engelmannii
Grows in cool ravines. Needles
prickly to the touch. Cones
papery, about 2″ long.

WHORTLEBERRY
Vaccinium scoparium
Small fine leaves, angular stems.
Grows in the forest, seldom
over 8″–10″ high. White flowers;
red, edible berries.

SAGEBRUSH
Artemisia tridentata
Woody bush with gray-green
leaves, common on open hillsides;
2′–3′ high. Pungent odor.
Not a true sage.

ASPEN
Populus tremuloides
Leaves showy because they dance
in the slightest breeze.
Trunks showy because so white,
similar to birch.

WILDLIFE

A long day of wildlife watching in Yellowstone during early May, while snow still holds animals fairly concentrated, will range from sighting elk, buffalo, moose, deer, bighorn sheep, antelope, coyote, and grizzly bear to a possibility of rare species like cougar or wolf and to small, solitary species such as porcupine, badger, marten, and muskrat. Total individuals seen will number in the thousands, all of them free to roam, feed, breed, and die as part of the fabric of nature.

THE THREAT OF EXTINCTION

The continued existence of all park species has not been automatic. Probably no mammal holds more of the romance of pre-Columbian America than does the buffalo, or bison; yet had it not been for a remnant herd in Yellowstone, buffalo running wild would have disappeared from the United States by about the turn of the century, except for small herds held by a few ranchers on their private lands.

Buffalo were the mainstay of Indians throughout the whole mid-continent for centuries, so abundant that they once numbered in the tens of millions. Writing in his *Narrative of a Journey Across the Rocky Mountains to the Colorado River, 1834–1839,* J. K. Townsend described the Platte Valley as "covered with one enormous mass of buffaloes." Another early account tells of the steamer *Stockade* stopped dead in the water of the upper Missouri River by buffalo, her engines helpless against the black mass of swimming bodies. Hours passed before the herd finished crossing the river and the boat could proceed. Later, trains were similarly blocked. These great herds belonged to the plains. Smaller herds ranged eastern America from Hudson Bay to Georgia.

French *voyageurs* in Canada had referred to these New World native cattle as *"les boeufs,"* and from this came the Anglicized "buffle," "buffelo," or "buffalo." "Bison" is from the scientific name, *Bison bison,* and is used interchangeably with "buffalo" as a common name. By the late 1820s buffalo robes were the prime trade item of the fur business. On the upper Missouri white traders offered Indians three cups of ground coffee, six cups of sugar, or ten of flour in exchange for a single skin. Shipment to New Orleans via the Missouri and Mississippi ballooned from 850 robes in 1803 to 199,870 in the peak single year, 1828; and this was just the first stage.

47

Moose browsing willow

Buffalo at hot spring

When buffalo robes lost fashion, hides took over the market: a new tanning process had been developed. One Cimarron hunter estimated his personal kill at 20,500 buffalo during the hide heyday. Another hunter shot nearly six thousand in a single autumn—so many that he went deaf in his right ear from the roaring of his Sharps rifle.

Hunting became epidemic, and "sport" turned into extravagant slaughter, in the early riverboat days, intensifying a few years later with the arrival of trains. Kills wildly exceeded the needs of the camp for meat or trophies, for, as a hunter of the 1840s expressed it, a man could scarcely "resist the temptation [to kill] when the whole earth, it seemed, was a surging, trembling, mass of these animals." As railroad tracks reached the buffalo country, special excursion trains were advertised at ten dollars a trip to see and shoot buffalo. Soldiers at frontier posts added to the carnage by holding contests to see who could kill the most buffalo, with tongues accepted as proof of fatal shots. A Fort Dodge officer wrote with pride that his men had killed 112 buffalo "from the same spot in less than three quarters of an hour."

"Bone pickers" played the last act in the wanton drama—professionals who gathered buffalo bones by the wagonload and stacked them along railroad lines to await shipment, or even ahead of rails, where track would soon be laid. Homesteaders needing cash also gathered bones. Oliver Nelson, a settler on the Oklahoma panhandle, spoke of picking up three thousand pounds of bones in an hour, or "sometimes in twenty minutes," and selling them for $7.50 a ton. Old, bleached bones went into the manufacture of china and were ground as meal for fertilizer. New bones produced calcium phosphate, used to neutralize acids in cane juice as it was refined into sugar.

Horns were marketable, too, for knife handles and buttons. "Once [a] buyer offered me 50¢ a pair for all the buffalo horns I would bring in," Mr. Nelson recalled. "I drove a day and picked up 300 pairs of good ones. . . . I also brought back several pounds of bullets I'd picked up where the carcasses lay, and brother George melted them down."

By mid-century the thunder that had rolled from buffalo hoofs like an endless drumbeat was silenced forever on the plains. Only dusty wallows and bones not yet gleaned remained to speak of what had been—and also one last wild band of buffalo that had escaped annihilation because of its remote location: Yellowstone. In 1885 the naturalist George Bird Grinnell wrote in the *New York Sun*: "There are, to my positive knowledge, not more than 700 bison . . . left. . . . About 180 are in Yellowstone . . . [and] I have heard that twenty head were killed [there] by a party of English tourists." Probably Grinnell's figures are inaccurate. An actual population census is unlikely at that time. But his point is all too true: only Yellowstone harbored buffalo still free on their native range. They were mountain buffalo, slightly smaller than plains buffalo and warier, faster on their feet, darker in color, and with finer, curlier hair.

In 1898 the park superintendent estimated Yellowstone's buffalo as down to fifty head, having dropped in a quarter century from a population that probably actually numbered about one thousand head. Hunting had been allowed in the first years after the park's establishment, and poaching continued even after Congress voted to stop all shooting, whether for sport, table use, or the commercial market. By 1902 bullets were no longer an active threat, but herd size had dwindled so drastically that inbreeding loomed. To solve this new problem the Park Service brought in buffalo from Texas and Montana where ranchers were trying to domesticate them. The new arrivals, of plains buffalo stock, were corralled first at Mammoth and later in the Lamar Valley. They were used to breed with the wild buffalo of the park and assure survival.

These efforts succeeded. Today buffalo in Yellowstone, and in refuges beyond park boundaries, again crop the grass of open ranges and squirm their great bodies against patches of bare earth, dust bathing. Old bulls stand with a massive solidarity that suggests permanence—until one remembers how close the species came to disappearance.

A similar tale of salvation because of sanctuary in the Yellowstone region belongs to a wholly different type of creature: the trumpeter swan, largest waterfowl species in the world. Their wing span stretches nine feet, about the same as the length of a buffalo. Once these swans whitened the skies from the Arctic to the Gulf Coast, and their ringing call orchestrated the flyways, but by 1932 only sixty-nine trumpeters could be counted in conterminous United States. They had been turned into powder puffs, swansdown, feather decorations, and quill pens. Hudson's Bay Company alone marketed 17,671 swan skins in London between 1853 and 1877.

Trumpeter swans

The nesting ground of the last United States trumpeters lay just outside Yellowstone's west boundary, in the Red Rock Lakes of Montana. In 1935 the area was set aside as a wildlife refuge, and nature set about healing itself. By the end of the 1960s trumpeter swan counts approached four or five thousand. They were still a rare sight on most of the continent, but their future seemed to be assured. Perhaps fifteen pair were staying the year around in Yellowstone, joined each spring by smoke-gray puffs of cygnets, three to six to a brood, and additional swans nested in Jackson Hole and at Red Rock. Winter counts increased to one hundred in Yellowstone, with flocks of up to fifty at a time on the Yellowstone River. But with the 1970s came new alarm. For unknown reasons, only three cygnets were raised in Yellowstone in 1971, and counts were also down at Red Rock Lakes. Trumpeter swans may be joining the roster of threatened bird species, a sad list that already includes bald eagles, ospreys, and pelicans.

PREDATORS

In the early years of the park, an effort was made to compensate for the slaughter of previous decades. Wildlife was protected even from itself, in an extension of man's urge to safeguard domestic flocks and herds. Predators were considered "bad" and were killed. Their role in culling weak animals and maintaining wild herd balance was not realized. The fact of predation was noticed, but not the value that stemmed from it.

Early park superintendents reported an abundance of wolves and coyotes in the early 1870s, but a decade later their reports listed these animals as scarce; elk carcasses poisoned with strychnine and used as bait had taken their intended toll. Cougars, or mountain lions, were also pursued with the intent of eliminating them as a species. In 1908 only one cougar was found and shot, and that year's report comments that it "no longer is necessary to keep the pack of hounds purchased in 1893 for the extermination of mountain lions. . . ." The dogs were advertised for bid, and sold.

The killing of other predators went on. During the decade ending in 1926, 134 wolves were trapped and poisoned or shot in the park. At that time all wild creatures were seen from a human viewpoint. An official park book for 1929 neatly divides the discussion of wildlife into "Man's Interest" and "Use to Nature." Golden-eye ducks are "not considered a choice bird for eating," although they are "food for flesheaters." Cassin finches are a "friendly little bird with pleasing color and a rich song, thought to destroy fruit blossoms

Coyote

occasionally when not breeding." They also "aid in control of insect life." Badgers are "sullen and ugly seeming." Grizzly bears are "important destroyers of mice and ground squirrels."

Today wildlife interrelationships are recognized as complex, and wise management has become nonmanagement, a blending back into the long ages when man was one species among many, one part of the whole but not dominant. This requires vastness and wildness which are seldom available today, yet which are the very qualities Yellowstone was set aside to preserve. Given this new treatment—which is nontreatment—nature is restoring itself. Planteaters and flesheaters are resuming their old roles and interrelationships.

Cougar, lynx, bobcat, and wolverine are still seen only one every few years, even by hikers and researchers who penetrate Yellowstone's most remote corners, but these are secretive species seldom seen anywhere. Their present numbers cannot be accurately compared with primeval numbers because nobody can find them to count them accurately. Coyotes are again a common sight, mousing sagebrush slopes and patrolling riverbanks for ducks, and wolves give promise of coming back. A few years ago the last wolf was believed to have been shot, but now they are occasionally seen in the back country—lone wolves for the most part, but also an occasional small group including pups. The numbers still only faintly echo the former wolf packs, but they represent a hope, for within a wilderness ecosystem man has no reason to fear wolves. Few animals equal their shyness or fleetness; the least scent or sound of man, and wolves are gone, bounding through underbrush or disappearing over a ridge. Some travel nearly fifty miles a day to find food. When they attack they select animals in poor condition—and for the herds of elk or deer this loss of the weak means better feeding and breeding.

Yellowstone wolves have an esthetic role, as well, one nearly forgotten because it is so rare throughout the world today: the great throbbing, quivering harmonics of their howl. The sound belongs so basically to the music of the wild that with the wolf voice stilled a major melody is missing. The bugling of elk, the joyous songfest of coyotes, the clamor of mating geese and sandhill cranes and trumpeter swans are mere practice sessions compared to the mastery and resonance of wolves' wild chorusing.

ELK

For at least twenty-five thousand years, to judge from fossils, elk, or wapiti, have roamed the Yellowstone country, a distinctly New World species that crossed from Asia by land bridge during the ice age. Once elk ranged over nearly the whole continent, coast to coast and southward almost to Mexico, but by the early 1900s only an estimated seventy thousand of the animals were left in all of America, with perhaps half of them in the Yellowstone region.

Elk herd in fall

Presently a herd of about one thousand stays the year around in the vicinity of the Firehole, Madison, and Gibbon rivers, and three other herds move at least partly out of the park as autumn storms howl their yearly prelude to winter. About four thousand elk migrate southward into Jackson Hole, where the overall snow depth is less than in Yellowstone and a wildlife refuge assures wintering ground. Another thousand move along the Gallatin drainage of the Yellowstone River, and the largest of the park herds ranges in and out of the park along the rest of the river's drainage. About twenty-five or thirty-five hundred elk in this herd are now expected to winter inside park boundaries on the Lamar and Yellowstone rivers, and another three to five thousand may periodically move outside near Gardiner.

In some ways elk are particularly central to man's growing knowledge of Yellowstone wildlife. They are the most abundant and therefore the most conspicuous of all the park's large animals. In sheer total poundage they outnumber all other grazing animals combined, and therefore they have the greatest effect on park vegetation. Presumably to help the elk herds, war was initiated against predators in the park's early days. Yet the loss of natural wintering ground to cattle and sheep and horses went uncorrected until 1932, when the north boundary was changed to follow more closely an ecological line and allow elk, deer, and antelope the wintering ground they had used for millennia. Even so, winter kills remained heavy and were thought to reflect a range problem. Correction of the losses was sought through herd reduction. Virtual firing lines of hunters shot elk migrating out of the park in fall, and inside park boundaries elk were trapped for shipment to zoos and stock ranges elsewhere.

Today the human viewpoint has changed. The national park is large enough, and the years have been long enough, for man to observe wild animals in wild situations and slowly accumulate knowledge that is overturning previous opinion. Fluctuations in herd size are now seen as normal for elk. Die-off during occasional exceptionally severe winters is a natural means of population control. For example, in 1969–70 snow came late but piled deep and lasted long, and possibly as many as one quarter of the Madison herd met death. Most were calves that died of malnutrition—sad to the human mind, but of little consequence to the herd. The strongest calves survived, and the weak would be replaced by the new spring births. Similarly, the bulls that had been most active during fall breeding were harder hit by winter than were the younger bulls, not yet dominant. Harems take time! The stalwarts of a rutting season have no time to feed well and lack the energy reserves needed for winter. But this, too, is an advantage. It assures different bulls and new genes when the time is right for the next rut and the perpetuation of the herd.

As for the dead, their loss is merely individual and therefore in nature's system of no importance. What counts is that their flesh contributes to the ongoing life of the total wildlife community. Most die because of snow and cold and the difficulty of getting food. A few are overtaken by predators, chiefly grizzly bears, and so are sped to the destiny that awaited them in any case. Both ways are completely natural, and both are a source of life for flesheaters from bears and wolves and coyotes to mice and magpies. Within forty-eight hours every trace of flesh on an elk carcass disappears.

FISH

Predators were "bad," elk were "good," and fish existed for man's frypan—or so human attitudes categorized wildlife. To supply more fun and food, Yellowstone waters were stocked with nonnative species of fish, beginning in 1901 when an army hatchery opened at West Thumb. By 1953 there were six cutthroat trout egg collection stations on Yellowstone Lake and additional operations on Grebe Lake (for grayling) and Trout Lake (for rainbow). The undertaking was large in scale and complicated. Fish migrating upstream were caught in weirs and stripped of eggs; bears were drawn by the smell; and electric fences and guard dogs were brought in to protect both eggs and men from the bears—all of this to "help" nature.

In 1953 the hatchery and stocking programs closed and effort concentrated instead on understanding the full web of relationships that center on Yellowstone's native trout, grayling, and whitefish—for humans are not the only fishers. Pelicans colonizing the Molly Islands of Yellowstone Lake need hundreds of thousands of fish per year. Ospreys and bald eagles plummet from the sky to fish the park lakes and streams, and mergansers paddle and dive after fish. Otters and minks and grizzly bears swim and wade the shallows, also fishing. The web thus affects terrestrial as well as aquatic life.

New angling regulations have now been drawn up to assure all park visitors a chance to see the fish and the associated wildlife, not just those who come equipped with rod and reel. The regulations also protect the particularly vulnerable native cutthroat trout and grayling—strains that have persisted genetically pure despite man's tampering with the ecosystem. The largest population of native cutthroat trout in the world swim in Yellowstone Lake, the river above the Upper Falls, and the lake tributaries to the crest of Two Ocean Pass—fish so genetically pure, in water so pure, that they are spoken of as museum specimens in museum streams. Admittedly, any fishing fits inconsistently into other stated park wildlife goals of observing without disturbing, but the new fishing at least pivots on an interest in fellow creatures beyond their place on a dinner plate. Seasons and limits are stringent for the well being of the fish and of the many species dependent on them, and anglers are urged to release fish instead of keeping them. (The survival rate is about 96 percent of fish caught on flies or spinning lures because the hook catches in the mouth, whereas with bait, the hook is usually swallowed at least into the throat, and fewer than 50 percent of released fish survive its removal.)

Sixteen species of fish now live in park rivers and lakes, seven of them sought by human anglers: the native cutthroat trout, grayling, and whitefish and the introduced rainbow, brown, lake, and brook trout. The other species

Cave Falls

White pelicans

are dace, chubs, shiners, sculpins, and suckers—fish spurned by man, but fed upon by larger fishes and by birds. Thermal activity seems of little consequence to them. Hot water bubbles from springs in the bottom of several Yellowstone trout streams and lakes, and overflow from geysers pours in along the Firehole River, in the Shoshone Geyser Basin, and at West Thumb. Fish seem unaffected, except beneficially as warmth lengthens the growing season of organisms upon which they feed. Even trout, which are notoriously cold-water fish, swim within a few feet of hotspring water pouring at 200°F. into a stream. The iciness of the water as a whole dissipates the heat before its effect can spread much beyond the point of entry.

BEARS

Two kinds of bears roam the Yellowstone wilds: black bears, the most commonly seen, and grizzly bears, larger, warier, and more ferocious if angered. These two species above all other wildlife epitomize both the delight and the dilemma of coexistence, man with beast. No sight elicits greater comment, or exposure of film, than a sow bear with cubs. At the same time, injury and even death have come from encounters between man and bear.

The first recorded attack occurred in 1907 when a park visitor chased a grizzly cub up a tree and prodded it with an umbrella, whereupon the man was himself "prodded" into eternity by the enraged mother bear. Nearly all subsequent trouble has stemmed from comparable human folly although sometimes not the direct foolishness of the person injured. A sort of "corporate folly" developed as soon as people started coming to Yellowstone for its spectacular sights. Awareness of belonging to nature dimmed, and in its place grew a lordly illusion of being able to dictate terms and then sit and watch. Actually, mere physical presence makes man a participator—and usually a disrupter—unless he takes deliberate steps to play the role of onlooker wisely.

With people came garbage. By the 1890s hotel dumps had become a new source of easy food for bears, a notoriously omnivorous animal. Ants, grass, an elk carcass, potato chips, chocolate cake—any organic substance and some that aren't seem fit for a bear not only to eat but to thrive on. Watching bears dine became another park sight, along with geyser eruptions and thundering waterfalls. Beginning in 1919, feeding stations were supplied with garbage and staffed by rangers who gave evening talks about the wilderness while bears acted as backdrop, as many as thirty or forty appearing out of the forest, blacks and grizzlies, drawn by the promise of jam jars to lick and steak bones to paw through.

Wisely, the showmanship of bear feeding was stopped in 1941, but the handling of the garbage has taken more than mere decision. Of necessity dumps continued, away from human gaze but known to bears. By the end of the 1960s park garbage was amounting to nearly seven thousand tons per summer season, and several generations of female bears had passed on to their young a knowledge of the new-style "wilderness" living. They had been led to dumps and taught the techniques of raiding garbage cans and campers' supplies, and of roadside begging. Such unnatural association with man gave rise to injuries, for bears are not Winnie-the-Poohs or wise Smokeys or Gentle Bens—they are touchy animals. When their sense of individual space is violated, when cubs seem endangered, when a dozing bear is disturbed in its daybed, when cookies are offered and then teasingly withdrawn—any such cause may lead a bear to cuff or bite or maul, in defense or offense or retaliation or beastly frustration.

Nevertheless, the ratio of injury to total park visitors is only one per 1.5 million in areas with both black bears and grizzlies, something like a 0.00007 percent chance of trouble. In Yellowstone there have been only two deaths from bears in the century since the park's establishment. Compare these statistics with highway injuries, drownings, falling while climbing mountains, or hunters accidentally shooting each other, and bears seem relatively innocuous.

Yet, perspective cannot negate problems, nor does the fact of mass human foolishness as an underlying cause eliminate possible future individual pain or tragedy. Solutions are needed, and are actively under way. In Yellowstone, garbage cans have been bear-proofed by replacing old-style lids with swinging doors like those on mailboxes—a system that so far has foiled the bears. Open dumps have been replaced by incinerators. Campers are not only urged, but required, to keep food in tightly closed containers, plastic or tin, stored inside car trunks, not left out as accessible temptations. Bears panhandling by the side of the road are removed to park hinterlands, and humans abetting their bad habits by offering handouts are subject to fine.

In some cases campgrounds may be relocated out of the main travel routes of grizzlies, or closed during the weeks when feeding patterns draw bears to particular locations. For example, the campgrounds at Canyon and Fishing Bridge happen to be in areas favored as smorgasbords soon after

Black bear

bears have left their winter dens. Rodents and plants with thick bulbous roots are abundant, and can be dug simultaneously. Later in the year these foods lose their urgent appeal.

Similar management to fit man's activities to the entrenched habits and needs of the bears might call for temporarily closing a trail that passes through patches of ripe huckleberries, or along a stream thick with spawning cutthroat trout, or a mountain forest where whitebark pine nuts are ready to be feasted upon. Possibly campgrounds will be enclosed with fences to keep bears out, or ringed by sonic barriers objectionable to bears but undetectable by the human ear.

About 500 black bears and 250 grizzlies make up the Yellowstone bear population. The grizzlies are especially valued because they have few retreats left in conterminous United States. Originally the species roamed from the Arctic Circle into Mexico and from the Pacific to the Mississippi, but today only about one thousand grizzlies are left in the forty-eight states, with Yellowstone safeguarding the largest number. Alaska and western Canada have sizable undisturbed populations; and in conterminous United States Glacier National Park is second to Yellowstone as a last haven, and other wild parts of Montana, Wyoming, and Idaho support lesser numbers of grizzlies.

Shy of man unless spoiled by the false lure of food, most grizzly bears stay in the back reaches of the park, occasionally seen far in the distance foraging a hillside or crossing a late spring snowfield to feed on carrion. They are larger than black bears, weighing an average of six hundred pounds for a mature male compared to around three hundred for a black bear. (Alaska brown bears are usually considered one kind of grizzly; they weigh up to fifteen hundred pounds.) Color varies greatly for both bears, much as human hair comes in widely differing colors. Black bears as a species may be black or brown or cinnamon or honey or any shade between. Grizzlies also range in hue, but tend toward a silvered, "grizzled" tinge especially across the shoulders. Compared to black bears they are humpbacked and have a dished face and long snout. Grizzlies stand as high as seven or eight feet when they rear on hind legs; blacks are seldom more than about five feet.

SEEING PARK WILDLIFE

Off season is better than summer. Snow forces herd animals into low elevations and concentrates them where food is most freely available. The bugling and antler-banging of bull elk during September and October rut prompts awareness of the primeval miraculously lingering in our modern age. So does the chance to sit peaceably among a band of fifty or sixty bighorn ewes and lambs grazing on MacMinn Bench near Mammoth, or the sight of buffalo surrounded by snow, warming themselves at steam vents along the Firehole River. (Observe without intruding, however. Each species tolerates only a certain approach; if a man crosses that invisible barrier the animal will usually move away, but will occasionally charge.)

In summer most elk migrate to high meadows, but enough linger at lower elevations to make it worth watching for them in any green swale. If they are lying down only their ears may show, small twin pennants of dark brown; or it may be the sound of sloshing water that signals the animals' presence as they cross a creek. Roadside meadows between Mammoth and Old Faithful, along the Madison River, and from Yellowstone Lake to the east entrance of the park are particularly promising places to look for summer elk.

Buffalo, like elk, head for high country when summer frees the range of snow. Outrider bulls and small bands, however, are occasionally seen along the Firehole and Lamar rivers, in Hayden Valley, and along the northeast shore of Yellowstone Lake between Fishing Bridge and Lake Butte.

Moose are likely in Swan Lake Flat and Willow Park (north of Norris), along the Lewis River, between Fishing Bridge and the east entrance, and in Hayden and Lamar valleys. Largest of the North American deer family, moose equal horses in size, weighing up to nearly half a ton and standing five or six feet at the shoulder. Usually they stay solitary or rove in bands of from two to four. They can feed belly-deep in a marsh, or even submerged, probing the bottom muck for plants thirty or forty seconds at a time, then lifting dripping heads to breathe and chew before nosing after more. Often moose browse willows, and occasionally one will place its muzzle over a

Bull moose

sapling and press until the tree breaks, then feed on upper branches otherwise beyond reach. In winter Yellowstone moose rely heavily on subalpine
fir needles and twigs. (A Michigan study found that it takes about sixteen
hundred pounds of plant food per year to support a single bull moose.)

Mule deer are likely to be seen anywhere in the park, especially early and
late in the day. In winter they throng by the hundreds on the flats below
Mammoth. Bighorn sheep are often seen on Mount Washburn in summer
and on MacMinn Bench (near Gardiner) in winter. Antelope are likely the
year around on the sagebrush hummocks in the Gardiner vicinity and in
Lamar Valley. Coyotes and bears may be anywhere. Grizzlies are seldom
visible from the road in summer, but are often seen in spring when they
prey on weakened elk and scavenge winter-killed carcasses. (Back-country
grizzly areas, together with human precautions, are listed in the hiking section of this book.)

A deeply significant value of Yellowstone wildlife centers in the fact that
all species naturally belonging in the park are still there—a situation that has
vanished practically everywhere else in conterminous United States, and
throughout most of the world. Large mammals attract the most attention,
but a host of others are equally engaging. Red squirrels scold from tree
trunks and bombard trails with cones. Chipmunks and golden-mantled

ground squirrels scamper through grass and sage and forest, easily told apart because chipmunks have a stripe through the eye and ground squirrels do not. Picket pins, or Uinta ground squirrels—an unstriped brown-gray—watch from burrow mouths, when disturbed, or sit tall and utterly motionless. Their name comes from their supposed resemblance to the stakes used to picket grazing horses.

With luck, beaver may be seen, or perhaps heard on a moonlit night slapping their broad flat tails against the water surface to warn of possible danger. Far more common, and often mistaken for beaver, are muskrats. They look similar swimming along with just nose tip and beady eyes showing, but muskrats are much smaller than beaver and have quite ordinary long, narrow, rodent tails. They build lodges much like those of beaver, or sometimes take over an inactive beaver lodge. Shrews hurry nervously about the forested lands and meadows, searching for grubs and insects to satisfy their voracious appetites. Mink patter along the edge of streams. Occasionally a marten may look down from a pine branch, eyeing a hiker or camper. Marmots—large woodchucks native to the West—whistle from rocky slopes, and pikas, or rock rabbits, frequent similar locations. Once in a while porcupines will lumber into sight, and their presence is marked by bare patches on tree trunks where they have gnawed bark.

The varied habitats of the park attract birds from sparrows to eagles, from sandpipers to swans. Meadowlarks carol from the branch tips of sagebrush, and migrating warblers and bluebirds brighten the somber black-green of conifer forests. Yellowlegs patrol lake shores and fly in raucous alarm at the approach of man or canoe. Ravens brush black circles onto the blue and white canvas of sky and clouds. Canada geese graze riverbanks and swim in a ballet of flawless Vs. Ospreys weave scraggly nests in pines and on rock pinnacles, and their high soaring and hovering, followed by a plunge for fish and a lift to soar and hover again, give the park an almost nostalgic flavor of wild freedom.

Arctic three-toed woodpecker

Enjoying the Park

Roaring Mountain

TRIPS BY CAR

Entrance Roads: The road into the park from Gardiner and on through the Lamar Valley to Cooke City, the only road plowed during the winter, is open all year. Beyond Cooke City it is usually snowed closed and left unplowed from October until May. Winter also closes the east, south, and west entrances to the park. Snowmobiles (private, rental, and tour) travel from West Yellowstone to Old Faithful and Canyon, and also into the park from the south entrance, following snowed-in roads. No cross-country snowmobile travel is permitted, in order to protect land and wildlife.

Season: Ideal months for visiting the park are May and September into mid-October. Most roads are open, weather is usually mild, and colors are vibrant. Wildlife is abundant and easily observed. Traffic is light, and crowds are nonexistent. Facilities are limited; check regarding hotels, campgrounds, meals, groceries, and gasoline.

Winter brings a sense of purity and of vast wildness. Fair days with temperatures in the thirties alternate with gray, cheerless days or with howling storms and below-zero temperatures. The lowest temperature recorded in the park is −66°F., at West Yellowstone. While this is extreme, readings of −30° or −40° are not uncommon. Snowfall totals one hundred to four hundred inches, depending on the particular year and elevation, with two to six feet on the ground at a time. Opportunities for cross-country skiing are ideal for those who are experienced and properly equipped, but distances and weather can be formidable. The Lamar Valley remains accessible by road, replete with goldeneye ducks riding the river rapids and buffalo brushing aside snow with their huge, shaggy heads and reaching down to graze on unseen grass. The snowmobile trips offer a sure chance to see elk and buffalo, plus the spectacle of exquisite ice forms and of towering steam clouds in the geyser basins. Except for the guided snowbus tours, however, travel is rigorous, and the small snow machines are noisy.

Summer weather often includes thunderstorms, although they seldom last long. Three days out of four average sunny in July and August, slightly less than that in May and June and in September and October. Maximum temperatures occur in July and August, typically near 80°F., with 98° the highest recorded. Nights are chilly, usually dropping into the thirties and sometimes falling below freezing. An August night one year reached a low of 9°F.

For a chance to explore the park at the height of the summer season with minimal awareness of other people, try visiting major points of interest such as Old Faithful or Canyon at dawn, or walk the boardwalks through a geyser basin on a moonlit night, when sights are softened and sounds intensified. Turn off onto side roads—many of them one-way, specifically meant for leisurely enjoyment—and sample cut-of-the-way trails such as at Artists Paint Pots (about four miles south of Norris), or Mystic Falls (beyond Biscuit Basin), or Wraith Falls (east of Mammoth). Ninety percent of the park lies essentially untouched by man. From the air the roads and the crowds are mere threads on an immense tapestry of plateaus and forests and geyser basins and lakes. Something of the feeling of this pristine vastness can be sensed by getting even a little way beyond the pavement, and by picking the time of day, or the season.

THERMAL BASINS: Mammoth to Old Faithful and on to West Thumb (Map 1)

MAMMOTH HOT SPRINGS gush and seep from the earth with a daily flow of 700,000 gallons, each twenty-four hours adding two tons of new travertine to the already huge terraces that stairstep the mountainside. The figures are stupendous, but in keeping with Yellowstone statistics, for park waters as a whole bring hundreds of tons of minerals to the surface every day. Limestone underlies the Mammoth area, and as hot water mixed with carbon dioxide rises through this layer it acts as carbonic acid, dissolving the rock. The same process dissolves limestone in caverns and deposits it as stalactites and stalagmites, but on the terraces the rate is much faster than in caverns because of the heated water. Activity and formations on the terraces change as existing conduits are sealed over by travertine and new ones open, but the total flow from the springs stays remarkably constant. Indication of this is the steady volume of Hot River (east of the Mammoth chapel), water that issues directly from underground without flowing over the terraces. The whole of Terrace Mountain, rising two thousand feet above Gardner Valley, is built of hotspring travertine—proof of how immensely long the process has been going on.

Ice, as well as fire, has shaped the terrain. During the ice age, a glacier two thousand feet thick overrode Mount Everts and blanketed the Mammoth area, leaving only the top of Bunsen Peak rising clear. The hummocky slopes across from today's travertine terraces are typical glacier outwash, and CAPITOL HILL, the high knoll across from the chapel, is formed of debris dropped by the glacier as it flowed over a hot spring. Heat melted the ice, and rubble fell from the bottom of the glacier and accumulated around the spring. Water swept away the sand and silt, but pebbles, cobbles, and boulders piled nearly two hundred feet high, their bottom layer incorporated into the travertine of the ancient hot spring.

Trails lead to OPAL, MAIN, JUPITER, and other terraces active today. Nature trail leaflets are available from dispensers at the parking areas. A

Mammoth Hot Springs

short road loops HIGHLAND TERRACE (2 miles above Mammoth Inn and gas station). An outlet at this upper level suddenly became active in 1953, and within weeks fresh travertine had coated the terrace and was beginning to kill trees. Limber pines and Rocky Mountain junipers five hundred years old, as old as any trees in the park, were affected. Their great age is an indication of how long this part of Mammoth Terrace had been inactive. ORANGE MOUND was built into an abrupt knob perhaps fifteen or twenty feet high, and water continues to rise through its core and flow in an even sheet over its sides, adding still more travertine and further encasing the trees. LIBERTY CAP, a thirty-seven-foot pinnacle of travertine near the lower terrace parking area, was probably formed in the same way. Its name, given by the Hayden Survey, supposedly comes from a resemblance to the shape of the peaked caps worn during the French Revolution.

On the upper terrace a sinkhole that slopes about ten feet into broken travertine holds a pool of water scummed green with algae and fringed at the edges with grass. This is POISON SPRING. Carbon dioxide bubbles here so constantly that it kills birds that come to drink—sparrows, warblers, bluebirds, nuthatches, juncos, pine siskins, western tanagers. A total of 236 individual dead birds were counted during one study from May through November. There are so many, and their death is so dependable, that coyotes make daily rounds picking up the bodies during times of bird migration. Death Gulch, along Cache Creek in the northeast portion of the park, is a similar gaseous area, but with hydrogen sulphide instead of carbon dioxide. An 1888 report mentions six dead bears there, one elk skeleton, the bones of several small mammals, and many dead insects. The gas, nearly twice as heavy as air, hangs in the gulch, and hikers approaching the area sometimes experience severe headaches.

The MUSEUM at Mammoth features exhibits on human history and wild-life, plus an audiovisual presentation on the park's ecology. Beyond Mammoth the road climbs to SILVER GATE, a jumble of travertine formed by hot springs before the ice age began and now fallen as a landslide from high on Terrace Mountain. A short turnout loop allows leisurely inspection. Next comes GOLDEN GATE, cliffs of welded tuff with a vivid lichen growing on them. SWAN LAKE FLAT lies beyond, an open stretch of sagebrush dotted with a shallow pond. Try coming here at dawn, from Mammoth or Indian Creek Campground. Stop first to see the new day's light turn the steam at Mammoth Terrace a diaphanous, backlit pink; then drive the four miles to the flat. Moose or elk are likely to be seen, and perhaps a coyote singing its final song before trotting to its den to sleep away the day. There may be swans, and in spring and fall mallards and all three species of teal bring the ponds to life. Through June and July, Wilson phalaropes paddle in tight whorls, stirring up insects to feed on.

The BUNSEN PEAK road loops from the north end of Swan Lake Flat back to Mammoth (see Side Roads at end of this chapter). Three miles from the Bunsen Peak road a spur leads to SHEEPEATER CLIFFS, named for the Indians who lived there when the park was established. The cliffs are colum-nar basalt, a type of volcanic rock that formed columns as it cooled. Farther along the main road, WILLOW PARK forms a transition from moose to elk habitat. The wet north end has aquatic plants in addition to the willow and subalpine fir preferred by moose, while the drier south end furnishes grass for grazing elk.

Water from APOLLINARIS SPRING, named for a spring in Germany famed for its bottled water, is safe to drink but mildly laxative. Watch for elk in the meadows across the road from the spring.

OBSIDIAN CLIFF, also called Glass Mountain, has a weathered gray surface patched with pale green lichen, but where there are fresh breaks, the obsidian shines a lustrous black. Perhaps 150,000 years ago a slow-moving, viscous volcanic flow stopped here, forming the sheer cliff which served early Indians as a quarry for stone projectile points and knives. Obsidian has the same mineral constituents as rhyolite, but because it cools quickly its texture is fine and hard, like glass, and it is highly desirable for sharp-edged tools. In fact, obsidian from this cliff is found at both ancient and recent Indian sites as far distant as Ohio and the Mississippi Valley. The stone was evidently valued for its exotic aura as well as its utility, for it is often present in burials of obviously elite persons. Indians may have made long pilgrimages to Obsidian Cliff to quarry stone for their needs, or tribes living close to Yellowstone may have cut the obsidian, then traded it across the hundreds of miles. Nobody knows. Identifying the exact source of the obsidian is possible because each flow has individual mineral characteristics that can be determined through a process of neutron activation.

ROARING MOUNTAIN earned its name in 1902 when fumaroles became unusually active, but since then the vents have enlarged and the noise has diminished. The steaming continues, however, and is an especially dramatic sight on frosty mornings and in winter when snow blankets the surrounding forest while the mountainside lies bare and primordial.

NORRIS GEYSER BASIN ranks as the hottest and most active thermal area in the park. Water temperatures within its earth may approach 706°F., the

Norris Basin in winter

highest point at which water can be distinguished from gas. A small MU-
SEUM there houses exhibits that explain thermal features and the life associated with them, and ranger-naturalists lead walks throughout the summer
season. Two separate trails thread the geyser basins, each providing a loop.
Boardwalks permit a safe approach to boiling springs and geysers. The exact
position of the walks is changed from year to year as the thermal activity
shifts. *Do not leave these walks.* Crusts are thin and easily damaged—and
they can plunge a careless human into scalding water. Animals occasionally
meet this fate. A spring in Lower Geyser Basin, for example, bears the
name Skeleton Pool after the buffalo and elk that have met death there
when ledges built out over the water broke. Such overhangs can be ten or
twenty feet wide without visible indication that they are unsupported. The
weight of an animal or a person stepping onto them breaks them immediately.

PORCELAIN BASIN (immediately below the museum) is named for its
pearly sinter, which adds great beauty to the spectacle of thermal activity
here. In addition, the pools of this basin are variously tinted and continually
changing. COLLOIDAL POOL is colored by the minerals silica and kaolin,
which are evenly mixed in its water. Others are colored by algae and bacteria, or by deposits of sulphur and iron oxide. Near the far end of the half-
mile loop trail, PINWHEEL GEYSER responds to current rainstorms and snowmelt, ceasing eruption when surface drainage floods too much cold water
into its opening, and other geysers show equally varying activity as indicated
by their names: WHIRLIGIG, CONSTANT, and SPLUTTER POT. An eerie,
steamy peace pervades this basin. Its location beyond the sight and sound of
cars eliminates distraction and fosters an awareness of the elemental.

Beyond the trees on the opposite side of the museum, BACK BASIN is worth
sampling even part way if time or energy precludes the entire 1.5-mile loop.
EMERALD SPRING gets its color from its yellow sulphur lining plus the clear
blue of its water, which combine to produce green. Usually the spring is
quiet, but occasionally its pool bubbles and spurts two or three feet high.
STEAMBOAT GEYSER is considered the largest geyser in the world, but its
mammoth eruptions are sporadic. Five were reported before 1911; then
none until 1961. Three years later there were twenty-nine major eruptions
lasting several hours, towering as high as 380 feet and roaring so loud that
men standing close to the geyser could not hear each other even by shouting.
Since then, however, activity has diminished. Perhaps the forceful eruptions
gutted internal plumbing, weakening or destroying the geyser at least temporarily. Only splashing eruptions continue, shooting twenty or thirty feet
every few minutes, but there is always the chance of a renewed major out-
break, any year, day, or hour. Dead trees, and ground rusty with iron oxide
and gray with silica, bear witness to the devastating power of Steamboat's
outbursts.

Below Steamboat Geyser is ECHINUS GEYSER, which shoots fifty to seventy-five feet high every hour or two. A shady hillside immediately above it offers a grandstand view while the pool fills and the preliminary splashings foretell the action to come. Juncos hop about the forest floor and chickadees chatter overhead. The geyser follows its own dictates in erupting —an elemental force beyond man's grasp and worth waiting for and witnessing for that reason, as well as for its unique beauty.

At NORRIS JUNCTION a road turns east, cutting across a forested plateau to join the eastside road near the Canyon of the Yellowstone. The 2-mile drive beside VIRGINIA CASCADES gives a view of the rushing, foaming Gibbon River as it makes a sixty-foot drop (one-way, looping back to the main Norris to Canyon road; enter from the west).

Norris was the location of one of the fourteen soldier stations during the park's army days, before the National Park Service had been created. The equivalent of today's ranger stations, these were occupied summer and winter—isolated, uncomfortable duty, with headquarters at Mammoth. Yet, if it had not been for the army's care, the park would have been lost to poachers and exploiters before civilian administrators were available. Even after the Park Service took over, rangers had to provide their own saddle horses and prove that they had feed enough to carry the animals through the winter. Army money was gone, and for years civilian funding was shaky. Still standing is the NORRIS SOLDIER STATION, built in 1908, which housed a sergeant, a corporal, and two or three men.

Park at ARTISTS PAINT POTS and follow the trail around the edge of the meadow and into the pine forest, allowing about half an hour for a look at a delicate, out-of-the-way thermal area. The first pools are colored cloudy blue by colloidal silica. The water at the bottoms of these pools is comparatively clear because the particles are in suspension, but at the surface the particles are fine, forming a colloid that gives the water a milky hue. Close by are red-brown pools, colored by iron oxides, and a clear green pool. A suspended substance may produce the green, or it may be caused by a yellow lining of the pool plus the blue of the water, which comes from the transmission of light rays. Runoff streams are patterned with strands of bacteria the size of matchsticks, some dull gray, others peach-colored. "Hotspring grass," *Panicum thermale,* grows along the edges of the channels. Up the hill, so many different sounds come from thermals within fifty feet of each other that the trail could be experienced with the ears instead of the eyes. A fumarole roars like a steam laundry releasing pressure. A bubbler with sand in its orifice splashes steadily. A viscous mudpot throbs slowly and evenly, like a well-adjusted pump, and a more fluid mudpot whispers like the first splattering drops of summer rain. From them all comes the tinkling of runoff water.

The trail to MONUMENT GEYSER BASIN, part of the same thermal system as Artists Paint Pots, begins beyond the Gibbon River bridge opposite the Paint Pots (see Hikes section).

At GIBBON FALLS water drops eighty-four feet over a broad, sloping ledge; then, after the leap, it winds sedately through green meadows to merge with the Firehole River and become the Madison River. At MADISON JUNCTION a road leads 14 miles to West Yellowstone. It winds along the Madison River and offers good chances to see elk and waterbirds, including trumpeter swans and great blue herons. NATIONAL PARK MOUNTAIN, close to the road junction, was the last campsite of the Washburn-Langford-Doane party during their 1870 exploration of the present park area. Here they discussed the wonders they had seen and the possibility of preserving them. The mountain is the edge of the Madison Plateau, an ancient lava flow. North across the river is PURPLE MOUNTAIN, a remant of one of the Yellowstone calderas, enormous chasms that formed when the roof of a magma chamber collapsed. The Madison MUSEUM highlights the exploration and early history of the park.

The FIREHOLE CANYON drive parallels the main road for 2 miles (one-way, for uphill travel, from north to south). The road is winding, following the bends of the dramatically beautiful Firehole River. The canyon walls are of rhyolite, roughly sculptured. Their appearance makes it easy to visualize great walls of molten rock moving slowly, with enormous slabs falling off as

Firehole Canyon

Elk grazing, Lower Geyser Basin

they cool. Lodgepole pines grow directly from boulders in the river, making an oversimplification of the usual claim that raw rock must be broken by frost action and pioneered by lichens and mosses before there can be soil enough for vascular plants.

The main road stays at water level for several miles along the FIREHOLE RIVER, in places separated from it by only five feet of grass or a slight rise and a fringe of young pines. Canada geese and trumpeter swans are likely to be seen the year around, and elk congregate by the hundreds in the meadows through winter and spring. To see such herds grazing at sunset, backdropped by the forest and by steam from Lower Geyser Basin, is to sense timelessness. The individuals have changed, but the herds remain; the continuity of the scene has been unbroken through thousands of years.

The FOUNTAIN FLAT ROAD forks from the main road at the northern edge of Lower Geyser Basin (see Side Roads section). LOWER GEYSER BASIN is "lower" in the sense of being situated downriver from the Firehole River. Topographically, Midway is an extension of Lower; only a forested mid-section separates the two.

FOUNTAIN PAINT POT, part of Lower Basin, is looped by a trail that leads to a hot spring with a runoff channel dyed orange and pink by algae and bacteria, a bubbling mudpot, fumaroles, geysers, and forested hummocks that are part of the moraine left by a glacier. This is one of the finest thermal walks in the park. (A Park Service guide leaflet is available at the beginning of the trail.) SILEX SPRING, a pool of clear, hot water, sizzles gently and continuously as bubbles the size of tennis balls rise from deep within its throat and break at the surface. FOUNTAIN PAINT POT occasionally shifts its position—including immediately after the Hebgen earthquake when it broke out into the parking lot. The mud comes from rhyolite broken into constituent minerals (feldspar and silica) by the action of hot water and gas and by mechanical wear as particles abrade one another.

The Hebgen quake radically and abruptly changed several features reached by the Fountain Paint Pot boardwalk. The temperature of LEATHER POOL rose from a warm 143° to a boiling 198°F., killing the brown algae that had lined it and prompted its name, and RED SPOUTER, which had been a fumarole, gained enough water to lob soupy red mud into the air from winter through late spring. In summer it now usually lapses back into mere steaming. MORNING, CLEPSYDRA, and FOUNTAIN geysers also changed. They are interconnected, and their pattern had been to erupt one after another, beginning with Morning, but the initial shock of the quake set off Morning and Clepsydra, quickly followed by Fountain. The three shot water and steam simultaneously for one day; then Fountain not only quit but went dormant for the next three years. Clepsydra spouted on, then died down when a shifting of heat rejuvenated Fountain; later it reverted to steady splashing. Meanwhile, the temperature of Morning lowered to 146°F., too cool to erupt. Standing on this part of the boardwalk allows a view of Clepsydra's sputtering on one side as SPASM GEYSER begins a series of bursts straight ahead and KALEIDOSCOPE GEYSER shows through the steam, with BIG BLUE GEYSER to its side. The four seem quite enough, but then comes the sound of major splashing as Fountain begins to play.

The FIREHOLE LAKE drive circles for 3 miles off the main road (one way; enter from the south). Entry is through pines, some of them killed when water shifted its course and drowned or overheated the roots, others with bare patches on their trunks where buffalo have rubbed to shed winter coats or where elk have polished their antlers. Such extensive rubbing by animals may contribute to keeping meadows open; enough trees are killed to affect the forest's overall invasion of a meadow. Beyond the trees are openness and the shine of water rivulets draining from hot springs and geysers. GREAT FOUNTAIN GEYSER, considered by many the most beautiful in the park, plays

Great Fountain Geyser

White Dome Geyser

from the center of a 150-foot pool ringed with concentric rims of sinter. The volume of its outpouring sets waves rolling across the pool and surging over the rim as a minor, circular waterfall. Close by, WHITE DOME GEYSER shoots from a twelve-foot cone built on a rounded dome of sinter. These two geysers—Great Fountain and White Dome—represent two distinct forms. Geysers of the fountain type spurt from pools in several bursts. The water from an eruption falls back considerably cooled and therefore takes time to reheat enough for another eruption. Cone geysers issue water from a vent too small for any significant amount to fall back in and affect the temperature.

At MIDWAY GEYSER BASIN a walk leads to GRAND PRISMATIC SPRING, the largest spring in the park, noted for its color as well as its size. The blue of its water and the pink of its algae are sometimes reflected in rising steam. Seeing Grand Prismatic in 1836, the fur trapper Osborne Russell wrote: "The water was of deep indigo blue boiling like an immense caldron, running over the white rock which had formed the edges to a height of four or

Grand Prismatic Spring

five feet. . . . The stream [cascading from Excelsior Geyser into the Fire-hole River] was of three distinct colors. From the west side for one third of the diameter it was white, in the middle it was pale red, and the remaining third . . . light sky blue. Whether it was something peculiar in the state of the atmosphere, the day being cloudy, or whether it was some Chemical properties contained in the water which produced this phenomenon I am unable to say and shall leave the explanation to some scientific Tourist who may have the curiosity to visit this place at some future period." Reflection of the colorful pools in the mist is the explanation accepted today, with the intensity of the effect depending on exact conditions. EXCELSIOR GEYSER is a crater three hundred feet in diameter, filled with churning water and constantly overflowing. It pours about four thousand gallons of boiling water into the river every minute, indicating a remarkable heat source: so much water, so hot, and so constant.

Almost four miles south of Midway, BISCUIT BASIN lies across the river from the road. It is a small basin and offers a chance to be relatively alone. From the bridge the impression is of a great expanse of glaring white heightened by the blue of the Firehole River and the green of the meadow. Sinter "biscuits" nearly four inches across used to edge pools here, but the Hebgen earthquake caused water levels to drop and destroyed support for the biscuits formed out over the water. They broke and sank. Others were broken by surges of water and thrown out ten or fifteen feet beyond the edge of the pools. A sinter ruffle that looks almost like pastry dough has remained intact. Boardwalks circle the basin. At the far side a 1-mile trail leads to MYSTIC FALLS, a cascade in a forested setting. It is not spectacular, but is ideal for a short walk and a sample of the peacefulness of Yellowstone.

South of Biscuit Basin lies BLACK SAND BASIN, similar in size and known for its springs and volcanic-glass sand, which formed as molten lava suddenly chilled and shattered on contact with ice. PUNCH BOWL SPRING bubbles within an aptly named rim of sinter, and a quarter mile farther on BLACK SAND POOL seethes an opalescent blue, its color caused by minerals held in colloidal suspension. EMERALD POOL and SUNSET LAKE are favorites of photographers because of their brightly colored algae and bacteria. The meadow, lush and green, is studded with the stark skeletons of dead trees. The trunks act as wicks, drawing up mineral-laden water which turns their lower portions chalk white. The stream here is IRON CREEK, misnamed because of its rusty color, which was once thought to come from iron oxide but actually results from algae and bacteria.

UPPER GEYSER BASIN has what is probably the world's most awesome group of geysers, including the renowned Old Faithful. Sixty-eight tons of minerals are poured daily into the Firehole River by the hot water gushing to the surface in this basin. Multiply this by the millennia of activity, and it is obvious that the entire area must be underlain with gigantic solution caverns holding the reservoirs of water that supply the various geysers. Eruptions of OLD FAITHFUL typically last from two to five minutes, and shoot out over ten thousand gallons of water. The long eruptions tower the highest and tend to come at slightly longer than average intervals after the preceding eruption. Preliminary surging and splashing signal the onset; then the great column lifts. The whole process has apparently remained unchanged at least since the 1871 Washburn-Langford-Doane Expedition first recorded this geyser's activity, so entranced they watched it nine times in one day. The large mound of Old Faithful, nearly two hundred feet across at the base and twelve feet high, was evidently built during an earlier period of activity. Its vents must have functioned then as a hot spring instead of a geyser, for geysers never build mounds of this type. Next the spring lapsed into dormancy that lasted long enough for trees to grow on the mound. Their needles and stumps, which became incorporated into the geyserite when activity resumed, are now eroding free. The prominent knobs near the vent of Old Faithful are stumps heavily crusted with geyserite.

Old Faithful

Boardwalks and a path lead around the Old Faithful mound, through the forest, and up to OBSERVATION POINT, which is high enough to give a panoramic view. Several geysers in this area have displays comparable to that of Old Faithful. GIANTESS seldom erupts, but once it starts it plays steadily for a day. As prelude it roars and shakes the ground so hard it almost seems the whole of Geyser Hill will be torn apart. VAULT GEYSER also pounds the earth, violently enough to be felt fifty feet from its vent; then its pool begins to pulse and boil, the eruption starts, and the pounding stops. (The eruption shoots only fifteen feet high. The pounding is the most impressive aspect.) GIANT and GRAND are the other huge geysers near Old Faithful. Giant went dormant in 1955, but like the others it is subject to rejuvenation—and because of its dramatic size it is hopefully awaited by a core of aficionados. The column of Giant shoots one million gallons of water 250 feet high, almost twice the height of Old Faithful. Its roots connect with fifty other known thermal units.

Grand Geyser erupts in a series of ten or twelve bursts reaching about two hundred feet, then lapsing into inactivity for eight to fifteen hours. This is the largest predictable geyser in Upper Basin. It is reached by a foot bridge across the Firehole River a half mile north of Old Faithful.

Boardwalks thread much of the basin, providing a safe approach to major features. Consult the Park Service guide leaflet to Upper Geyser Basin for current information. Features to watch for: BEEHIVE GEYSER, with a fair-sized cone, narrows inside to a nozzlelike eight-inch opening and consequently shoots water under great pressure, reaching 150 feet or more. CASTLE issues its column from an unusually large geyserite cone, an indication of a previous long, quiet period as a hot spring, the only way such a cone could form. GROTTO GEYSER, like Old Faithful, was apparently dormant long enough for trees to grow close to the vent. Their stumps are now encased in sinter, forming the "grotto" from which water erupts about half

Grotto Geyser

of the time, and sloshes and steams and hisses the rest of the time. Across the Firehole from Grotto is RIVERSIDE GEYSER, situated at the water's edge and jetting out over the river for seventy-five feet every six or eight hours.

From Old Faithful, heading on for West Thumb, the main road climbs to the continental divide at CRAIG PASS, 8,262 feet. Water from ISA LAKE, a small pond green with waterlilies, drains toward both the Atlantic and the Pacific oceans whenever there is enough to overflow. The west end of the lake drains into DeLacy Creek which curves and starts toward the Missouri and Mississippi rivers, while the east end of the lake empties into Spring Creek and starts toward the Snake River and the Columbia.

In the immediate area of the pass, subalpine fir dominates the forest. Below this elevation, lodgepole pine forest resumes and continues to the shores of Yellowstone Lake.

Isa Lake

THE NORTHERN PARK: Mammoth to the Lamar Valley (Map 2)

Settlement at MAMMOTH started with Camp Sheridan in 1886, a cavalry post located near Liberty Cap. In 1891 the name was changed to Fort Yellowstone and permanent buildings were constructed, including administrative offices and employee residences now used by the National Park Service. Portions of the fort were built as a showpiece, with Minnesota sandstone cut and marked for reassembly, and interiors finished in oak with ceramic tile facings for the coal grates and plate-glass mirrors for the walls. The army administered the park for thirty years, beginning in 1886 after a series of civilian superintendents had been unable to cope with the problems. In 1916 the National Park Service was created by Congress and took over care of the park.

The huge bare cliffs east of Mammoth belong to MOUNT EVERTS, a geologic layer cake. A sheet of ashflow tuff forms the top rim, and there also are layers of ashfall tuff, basalt, and andesite which intruded into marine sediments, baking them above and below. Mount Everts is named for Truman C. Everts, who wandered alone for more than a month in 1870 after becoming separated from the Washburn-Langford-Doane party. He was found near the mountains now named for him, emaciated and out of his mind but destined to recover fully.

Four miles from Mammoth, UNDINE FALLS breaks over the lip of an immense basalt flow and drops sixty feet down a series of stairsteps. A half mile farther, a short trail crosses through sedge and sagebrush to Lupine Creek and WRAITH FALLS. The falls slide over slick rock in a glade forested with pine, fir, and spruce. The rock is welded tuff, which jointed into columns as it cooled. Great slabs invite sitting and relaxing, listening to the creek and the wind and the birds.

BLACKTAIL POND, 6 miles from Mammoth, is the first of several small lakes ideal for watching waterbirds and occasional muskrats. Several ponds have silted in and turned into moist saucers filled with sedge, rich sources of food for grazing mammals and reminders of the ephemeral nature of geologic landforms, despite their seeming changelessness. Soils are glacial till— deep and well drained, and with so little available moisture that sagebrush instead of forest clothes the flats. Deer are frequent, hence the name of the pond, and elk often calve here in May and June while moving from winter range to the surrounding high plateau country.

BLACKTAIL PLATEAU DRIVE turns off 9 miles from Mammoth (for details see the Side Roads section at the end of this chapter). The main road between PHANTOM LAKE and FLOATING ISLAND LAKE (named for hummocks of water plants) follows the base of a cliff formed of welded tuff, a type of volcanic flow that makes sheer cliffs which spall off and cover their lower portions with talus. Charred bits of wood abound in the rock, indicating that this ashflow poured out over a forested land.

Mule deer

The PETRIFIED TREE, reached by a short spur road near Tower Junction, is caged by a heavy iron fence to protect it from being carried off piece by piece, as happened to a similar one on this same hillside. The remaining tree is an upright stump twelve feet high.

About 2 miles after turning north from Tower Junction toward the Lamar Valley, notice the GLACIAL KETTLES and ERRATICS. The "kettles," many of them now holding ponds, formed as great chunks of ice separated from a disintegrating glacier reaching out of the Beartooth and Big Snowy mountains. Silt and cobbles filled in around the chunks and insulated them, but in time they melted, leaving the hollows. Boulders that rode the glacier for miles were left stranded as the ice waned, hence the name "erratic" because they were transported out of their original positions. In this area almost every boulder has a Douglas fir tree growing close beside it. Shade and moisture, which foster seedling development, seem the most likely explanation, but why there is just one tree for each rock nobody knows.

The broad grassy valley across from the Lamar Ranger Station was used to raise hay as part of the BUFFALO RANCH operation, active from the 1880s through the 1930s. SODA BUTTE, five miles beyond the ranger station, is a travertine cone built by a hot spring that has now lost most of its heat. Enough remains, however, to keep the spring open and steaming in winter, and it is occasionally utilized by buffalo that wade along the stream, feeding on its grassy banks. Nine- and ten-thousand-foot peaks in the Beartooth Range wall the upper valley dramatically. Arcing from the north around to the east, the peaks include DRUID, BARRONETTE, and ABIATHAR peaks, AMPHITHEATER MOUNTAIN, THE THUNDERER, and MOUNT NORRIS. The cliffs are strongly layered, composed of successive sandstones, conglomerates, and breccias—stone pages from geology texts. In fall and winter clouds chill as they lift over the mountains, often dusting the peaks and ridges with snow and making the various layers even more conspicuous. In early summer waterfalls thread the cliff faces, pouring snowmelt into Soda Butte Creek.

From the valley the road climbs through a spruce forest to the northeast entrance of the park. It continues high through Cooke City (4 miles beyond the park boundary) and on to Red Lodge, one of the most spectacular alpine drives in the nation, banked with snow most of the year and with flurries of new white likely even in July and August.

CANYON: Tower Falls to Hayden Valley (Map 3)

About a mile and a half southeast of Tower Junction, a path leads from the road to an overlook of the canyon at CALCITE SPRINGS, the narrowest part of any of the four gorges of the Yellowstone River. The river lies five hundred feet below, with Douglas fir fringing its banks. Above them rise sheer cliffs, each layer a separate chapter of earth history: breccia, stream gravels, basalt, another layer of stream sediments, columnar basalt, lake sediments, glacial rubble—fire, capped by ice. Calcite Springs is a small thermal close to the river, the first one to be recorded by the Langford-Washburn-Doane exploration party. Deposits of nearly pure sulphur and of gypsum have built up around the vents, as well as the usual travertine or calcite. An oil seep, one of two in the park, stains the earth close to the hot spring. (The other is in a remote corner of Mirror Plateau.)

THE NEEDLE, a mile farther along the road to Tower, is a pinnacle of breccia 260 feet high. It stands alone beside the rushing blue and white water of the river, which dominates the foreground of the view. As backdrop, the vast openness of the Lamar country stretches beyond the gorge, its south-facing slopes vital as winter range for elk because snow melts and blows off them, leaving dried grass exposed and accessible.

Half a mile beyond the pullout for the Needle, OVERHANGING CLIFF flanks the road conspicuously with a thick flow of basalt that formed overlapping columns as it cooled and solidified. Above the basalt is a rhyolite flow, and below it is a gray bank of gravel, a former riverbed with its uppermost inches baked to red-brown as the molten basalt flowed over it.

Tower Falls

TOWER FALLS drop 132 feet over a wall of yellow stone to the milky blue river that snakes through the canyon. Minarets—"towers"—edge the brink. The rugged terrain in the vicinity of the falls allowed Indians traveling the Bannock Trail only one place to ford the river (close to the present Tower Falls parking area). John Colter is believed to have crossed here also as he came into Yellowstone to trap in 1807 after leaving the Lewis and Clark expedition. Signs of the Indian trail must have led him to this point, almost the only river crossing possible for a lone man on foot in winter. Ground squirrels abound on the slope below the parking area.

Between the falls and MOUNT WASHBURN, the road follows for a way beside a small stream that threads grassy banks in a pine forest setting, so perfect a scene it could be the model for a museum diorama idealizing mid-continent mountains. After the forest, the road crosses rolling flats where sagebrush contrasts with the green of grass and herbs, patterning the land with both color and texture. At this elevation (about nine thousand feet) sagebrush is considered a holdover from the Altithermal Period of seven thousand years ago when the climate was hotter and drier than it is now. Under those conditions, the plant invaded slopes far above the level where today's climate usually permits it to grow. Once established, however, it has survived—although its continuation on these high slopes appears precarious. The sagebrush is not readily replacing itself.

A short spur road beginning 8.5 miles from Tower Junction leads to a parking area and a sweeping view across the northern park to the Absaroka and Beartooth mountains. Whitebark pines at this elevation and particularly on toward the summit grow low and contorted, with branches growing only in the leeside protection of their own trunks. Subalpine firs darken draws and north slopes, where they are protected from prevailing winds. Their conical shape allows them to shed snow.

The mountain is named for Henry Dana Washburn, surveyor general of the 1870 expedition. On August 29 Washburn climbed the peak, 10,243 feet, and wrote of it: "I saw the canyon and the lake. There are unmistakable columns of steam in the distance. This is a glorious region." The following January, Washburn died of tuberculosis, which had quite certainly been aggravated by the Yellowstone trip. In a sense, the park cost him his life.

Five miles south of the spur road to the summit of Mount Washburn is DUNRAVEN PASS, elevation 8,850 feet, the highest point in the park reached by public road. It is named for the Earl of Dunraven, who came to Yellowstone to hunt in 1874 and upon his return to England wrote a book titled *The Great Divide,* one of the early works that called widespread attention to the beauties of the region. Tall spruce, fir, and whitebark pine give a feeling of deep forest at the pass, and beyond it are meadows studded with subalpine fir. Here is the finest flower garden of the park, with bluebell, columbine, geranium, forget-me-not, lupine, bog orchid, balsamroot, paintbrush—a gorgeous, long-lasting display.

Red squirrel

Uinta ground squirrel

Whitebark pine, Mount Washburn

A great gash in the earth; the sparkling, foaming river; and roaring water-falls are the distinctions of the GRAND CANYON OF THE YELLOWSTONE. The name of the river and of the entire park comes from the bare walls of this gorge. Indians called the lower river Elk River and the upper river "the one with yellow, nearly vertical walls." French fur trappers shortened and translated this to "Pierre Jaune" or "Roche Jaune," "Yellow Stone" or "Yellow Rock."

In the last half million years, vast lakes have twice formed behind lava flows near the head of the canyon, and twice they have overflowed, cutting the ancestral canyon. Glaciers, too, have played a part, filling the gorge and depositing an enormous overburden of sediments as the ice melted—sediments that were later flushed from the canyon by the river, with few remnants visible today. The best examples can be seen from Artist Point and on the Red Rock Trail. The large boulder in the forest near the rim of the canyon at Inspiration Point also arrived via the conveyor-belt action of ice, coming from a source at least twenty miles away. Other similar glacial erratics lie scattered among the pines.

The basic rock of the canyon is rhyolite which has been softened by hot gases and water and is therefore more easily carved than unaltered rhyolite. Thermal activity continues in the canyon even today, with examples visible from Artist Point or on the hike to Seven-Mile Hole, a favorite destination for fishing. Layers of basalt and of particularly hard rhyolite form the lips that the two great falls leap from, UPPER FALLS dropping 109 feet, and LOWER FALLS 308 feet. Rock slides and avalanches of snow and ice sculpture the sides of the canyon, and the river carries enough silt and stones to act as liquid sandpaper, continually deepening the channel.

Several overlooks offer views of the falls and into the depths of the canyon. Each viewpoint is different. INSPIRATION POINT, the northernmost viewpoint, offers an especially awesome look at the river and the best sense of the depth and abruptness of the canyon. Its bottom lies eight hundred to a thousand feet straight below. From GRANDVIEW the Lower Falls show plainly but far in the distance. LOOKOUT POINT provides the classic view of the Lower Falls on the north side of the canyon, as does ARTIST POINT on the opposite rim. A parking area and a half-mile trail allow access to the brink of Lower Falls; farther on, another parking area and path lead to Upper Falls. Standing at the brink of either gives a chance to see the enormous force of sixty-four thousand gallons of water per second curling over the falls in June. By autumn the flow lessens to about five thousand gallons per second. Both falls foam bridal-veil white, except at their crests where the color is green because of the way light refracts within the water. The yellows and oranges and rusts of the canyon walls and pinnacles come from the oxides of various minerals in the rhyolite.

Upper Falls of the Yellowstone

Several trails wind along the rim, and a few zigzag down the canyon walls. (See the Trails section of the next chapter; also, ask at the Canyon Visitor Center for a guide leaflet with a map and summary descriptions of the various overlooks and trails, and for the current schedule of walks led along the canyon rim by ranger-naturalists.) The MUSEUM in the visitor center features geology exhibits and a small gallery of canyon scenes.

Yellowstone Lake flooded HAYDEN VALLEY to a depth of three hundred feet in the first centuries after the glaciers retreated. As a result today's soils are rich with lake bottom sediments and nurture luxuriant vegetation. This in turn permits abundant wildlife. The road threads the valley for five miles, most of the way built on a terrace of the former lake.

The valley is named for Dr. Ferdinand V. Hayden, an eminent geologist who came to Yellowstone in 1859 with the Raynold Expedition, the first official government exploration into the park area. In the 1870s Hayden returned three times as head of major survey expeditions. The valley today is essentially as Hayden found it, the scene still compounded of the blue of the river, the green of meadows, the gray of sagebrush hills, the black of distant pines, the brown dots of grazing moose and buffalo, and the white of pelicans and swans. Much of the way the road leads close beside the YELLOWSTONE RIVER, flowing smooth and broad. Ducks and geese are almost certain to be seen, and often there are muskrats swimming cross current and rippling the water with a V as they progress.

Frequent pullouts allow stops off the road and a chance to step to the river bank and watch for the leaping and splashing of spawning cutthroat trout, eight to sixteen inches long. Females scoop redds in fine gravel and lay their eggs while the males swim alongside to fertilize them. The time of the spawning varies from year to year depending on weather. This part of the river has been closed to sports fishing because continual trampling was turning river banks from grass to mud, often with rotting fish as an additional blight. Also, from a purely scenic standpoint, an almost solid line of fishermen seemed discordant along a wild river in a wild valley. And waterfowl were suffering. The peace they need for nesting was lost, and the snarling of lines was a genuine hazard. A trumpeter swan was found dead with monofilament line choked around its long neck.

In early summer harlequin ducks, rare in the park as a whole, often bob in the riffles at Lehardy Rapids, about three miles north of Fishing Bridge, and much of the year as many as twenty or thirty trumpeter swans float on the river between canyon and lake. In summer they scatter to nest on small ponds, and while there they molt, so that they are unable to fly until new feathers grow in. Whistling swans join the trumpeters in fall, generally more secretive and holding farther out on the river, away from the road.

Watch for moose feeding on the marshy, emerald green bars and back eddies of the meandering river, and for grizzly bears on the distant sagebrush slopes. Never try to approach either animal closely; both species are

Yellowstone River

easily annoyed and may charge. (The same is true of any wild animal, any-where. Actual incidents are few despite frequent provocation, but when they do occur severe injury and even death are likely.)

SULPHUR CALDRON splutters below the road half a mile beyond the southern end of Hayden Valley. Its pH is 1.8, as acid as any in the park, about the same strength as the acid used in car batteries. Close by is the small MUD VOLCANO thermal group. Park and walk to see its features. A trail loops the hillside for a little over half a mile, with a guide leaflet avail-able at the beginning. Most of the way is forested, allowing an unusual sample of Yellowstone's life interspersed with its thermal wonders. Aster and yarrow bloom beside the trail, and birds or squirrels may be seen—or heard—in the pines overhead. Specific sights include several caldrons that seethe and bubble with escaping volcanic gases, and also examples of springs that have burst into activity within recent decades, such as BLACK DRAGONS CALDRON and SOUR LAKE. These two have an especially raw, primal look. The fissure of Black Dragons Caldron opened in 1948, shooting thick, black mud sixty feet into the air. Since then, vents have enlarged, the mud has become soupier, and the caldron has turned into a seething mudpot. At the same time that the Dragons Caldron grew active, the pale green, gaseous pond of Sour Lake began to enlarge, flooding and killing surrounding trees. A bright green species of algae, *Cyanidium calderium,* lives in this water. The same species, limited to acid springs no hotter than 131°F., is found wherever these unusual conditions of pH and temperature occur—Italy, Yellowstone, Hawaii, Southeast Asia.

Sour Lake

YELLOWSTONE LAKE AREA: Fishing Bridge to Sylvan Pass, also south to Lewis Lake (Map 4)

FISHING BRIDGE appeals to anglers who enjoy standing creel to creel, with rods and lines thrashing the water. Yet, despite throngs and chaos, an occasional fish is caught here, for the bridge spans the one outlet of YELLOWSTONE LAKE. The peninsula at the point where lake becomes river has one of the largest Indian archaeological sites in the park, doubtless because the sand beaches and the fishing were as attractive in the past as they are today. Ranger-naturalists lead walks to the lake shore through the summer. A MUSEUM houses displays on lake ecology, including mounted specimens of common birds.

Across the bridge, the meanders of PELICAN CREEK wind through sedge and willows favored by moose. Occasionally ten or more moose are seen here at one time. From Pelican Creek, the road to the park's east entrance skirts the north end of the lake, heading toward Sylvan Pass. At MARY BAY it passes a gravel beach lapped by waves and patrolled by sandpipers, yellowlegs, and other shorebirds, while California gulls flap and call overhead or sit, necks drawn close to their bodies, as if sculptured. Hot springs keep the bay partly open in winter, a refuge for swans, ducks, and geese, and steam vents back from the lakeshore melt snow from the meadow, leaving it open for grazing by buffalo through the winter. Other thermals steam from the bare mud of STEAMBOAT POINT, the toe of a ridge that reaches into the lake. Beyond it is a beach suitable for launching small boats. Swimming is not encouraged because the water is extremely cold and often rough, and exhaustion at this elevation (7,731 feet) can bring on sudden difficulty.

Three miles east of Steamboat Point a 1-mile spur road climbs LAKE BUTTE, a commanding overlook with Yellowstone Lake spreading blue through a black-green screen of pine and fir. The Teton Mountains are clearly visible nearly sixty miles to the south; closer, the Red Mountains and Mount Sheridan rise beyond the end of the lake. In the opposite direction, the Gallatin Range and Electric Peak mark the northwest corner of the park. The overlook offers an ideal respite from the effort of squeezing the park's long miles into the short hours usually available to see it, and the press of sharing scenic highlights with throngs of other people. A sense of limitless space and time pervades this spot, and man's sights and sounds seem far removed. Often thunderheads reflect in the blue of the lake, or on gray cloudy days an occasional shaft of sunlight darts across the water.

SYLVAN LAKE and ELEANOR LAKE lie two miles apart near SYLVAN PASS, each ringed by fir trees and backdropped by alpine peaks. At the pass (8,541 feet) slopes of andesite talus spill from the cliffs like a massive Japanese rock garden, totally lacking delicacy but perfectly embodying the simplicity and essential rockiness that underlie the genius of such gardens. The talus blocks spall off as frost forms in cracks, expands, and acts as a wedge, inexorably wearing down the cliffs. From the pass, the road drops fairly steeply 7 miles to the east boundary of the park.

Traveling south from Fishing Bridge, instead of around the north end of the lake toward Sylvan Pass, the road stays in sight of the water most of the way for 20 miles. It passes the massive Lake Hotel, built around the turn of the century to accommodate the era of the grand tour. At BRIDGE BAY a marina provides moorage for private yachts and serves as departure point for boat tours. (Check for current schedule and rates.) Rowboats are usually available for rent.

A 1-mile side road leads to NATURAL BRIDGE, a span of rock perhaps 150 feet high, arching above a tumbling creek. The bridge is not impressive, but is beloved as an oddity. GULL POINT offers a quiet 3-mile side road with a wooded hill part way and water the rest of the way—including quiet backwaters ideal for duck-watching. Fishing from the point is usually good from June until mid August.

YELLOWSTONE LAKE stretches 20 miles long and 14 miles wide. Its depth reaches to 339 feet in the South and Southeast arms, which are believed to be drowned valleys, and the average depth overall is over one hundred feet. In winter the lake freezes, becoming a sheet of white with only the tracery of animal tracks and the drift ridges of snow left to pattern its surface. By August, water temperatures generally warm to about 60°F. for the surface layers, while staying 42°F. at the bottom. Few trout live deeper than seventy-five feet because of the water temperature, which influences the availability of freshwater shrimp and insect larvae to feed on.

During its geologic history, Yellowstone Lake has drained to three oceans. It emptied toward the Pacific until the beginning of the Pleistocene, when the canyon formed. With its gorge as outlet, drainage then shifted to the

Marbled godwits, Yellowstone Lake

north, eventually reaching Hudson Bay. Later, as the continental glaciers waned, the Missouri River system developed and the waters of the lake began flowing through the Missouri River toward the Mississippi and the Gulf of Mexico.

The steam at WEST THUMB is visible for miles, issuing from a thermal basin directly at the lakeshore. A terrace of sinter reaches for nearly a mile along the lake and is as much as eighteen feet thick, its size an indication of greater thermal activity in the past than at present. The various features at Thumb include OVERHANGING GEYSER, which is rooted ashore but erupts from a sinter ledge that projects over the lake; FISHING CONE and BIG CONE, hot springs steaming from mounds out in the lake; and LAKESHORE GEYSER, twin craters that are submerged, and consequently unable to erupt, whenever the lake is high. Several hot pools at Thumb are notable for color. BLACK POOL combines the blue of exceptionally deep water with a burnt sienna lining of algae; ABYSS POOL is spectacularly deep and clear; and LAKESIDE SPRING bubbles a milky aqua blue and spills over into the lake, building a delta of white sinter about twelve feet into the water. Killdeer feed in the steamy meadows close by the hot pools, and meadowlarks occasionally add their clear song to the bubbling and popping of the springs. Monkeyflower and gentian contrast vivid yellow and purple with the glaring white of the sinter.

The MUSEUM at the Grant Visitor Center presents a wilderness theme with large photographic murals and "listening chairs" that feature the sounds of the wilderness. Lakeside walks are led by ranger-naturalists during the summer. A marina offers dock facilities and rental boats.

South of Thumb 3.5 miles the road crosses the CONTINENTAL DIVIDE at an elevation of 7,988 feet. Both the ascent and the descent are so gentle as to be scarcely noticeable if it were not for a sign pinpointing the spot. LEWIS LAKE, 4 miles farther on, lies separated from the road by only a fringe of trees, and not far from its south end LEWIS FALLS thunders, low, wide, and abrupt. Moose can be expected in the emerald mosquito meadows below the falls, and ducks ride the current of the river.

LEWIS CANYON forms a deep, dark gorge paralleled by the road for a mile and a half, its walls castellated and turreted. The river alternately threads the broad canyon bottom, leaving grassy sand bars, and foams over cascades.

The south entrance of the park is 10 miles beyond the falls.

SIDE ROADS

The BUNSEN PEAK DRIVE circles for 6 miles from Swan Lake Flat to Mammoth, for one-way downhill travel only (closed by snow except in summer and occasionally even then too wet and slippery for safe travel; ask current conditions). At its upper end the road crosses a sedge meadow, then skirts around the base of Bunsen Peak through sage and pine flats

Antelope

dotted with small ponds that are favored by ducks. The light green, or autumn gold, of aspen punctuates the somber black-green of the conifers. For about a mile the drive leads along the rim of SHEEPEATER CANYON with the Gardner River forming a ribbon of frothy white eight hundred feet below. OSPREY FALLS leaps 150 feet over a dark volcanic cliff.

The OLD GARDINER ROAD leads over the hill behind Mammoth Motor Inn. Much of the year it is snowed in or too muddy to travel; check current status. In late summer and fall there are good chances to see one hundred or more mule deer and possibly a few antelope, especially lone outrider bucks. The view is across jumbled terrain—blocks of rock and debris fallen from Terrace Mountain as a succession of landslides, now cloaked with grass and cupping small ponds where coots and ducks nest. Alternating layers of ancient sediments and volcanic flows show spectacularly on the face of Mount Everts, across the gorge. With binoculars, check MacMinn Bench for wildlife (see Trails section of next chapter).

At the base of the hill an unpaved road turns west from the park entrance, climbing and dipping over the hummocky sagebrush hills of the Stephens Creek drainage. Antelope can usually be seen from the car; or park and walk to enjoy flowers otherwise likely to be unnoticed and to explore ponds out of sight from the road, as well as to watch for wildlife. The ponds serve as drinking holes, the story of their use told by tracks and droppings even when the animals themselves are not around. Early morning and late evening are the best times to find deer and antelope.

Drive as far as the DEVILS SLIDE (out of the park, on the Stephens Creek road). It is a spectacular example of an ancient volcanic dike.

BLACKTAIL PLATEAU DRIVE, unpaved, parallels the main road between Mammoth and Tower Junction. It cuts across sage and grass hills and in and out of lodgepole pine and Douglas fir forests and aspen groves, 8 miles long, with abundant openness and beauty. Early summer brings spectacular displays of balsamroot, and autumn frosts turn the aspen to shining gold, the grass to a burnished red-brown. Watch for antelope, deer, and elk in spring and fall.

The FOUNTAIN FLAT ROAD threads the green meadows and pine forests of the Firehole River not far from Old Faithful. Elk are almost certain to be seen, and buffalo are present except in midsummer. Canada geese feed in the meadows the year around, waddling through high grass and occasionally stopping to lift their long black necks like periscopes, viewing the world beyond the grass stalks. The road ends in about 4 miles at Goose Lake, a shallow pond lying at the edge of lodgepole pine forests.

The BECHLER area, in the extreme southwest corner of the park, is reached from Ashton, Idaho, via State 47. It is not connected with the rest of the roads in the park—or with the crowds that throng the main park during the summer. Bechler offers a quiet corner with pine and aspen forest, carpets of wildflowers, and a rushing, spectacular river. At road's end CAVE FALLS forms a wall of foaming, thundering white water, and a trail leads beside the river to BECHLER FALLS. Camping is available just outside the park boundary. Notice the peak of the Grand Teton plainly visible from the approach road, distant but dramatic.

Canada geese

THE BACK COUNTRY

TRAILS

Roads lead to the major scenic attractions of Yellowstone, but beyond the pavement lie lakes and waterfalls and thermal basins, peaks and meadows and *space* reached only by trail.

Many trails are better suited to riding than to hiking. The park is big for a man on foot, and some trails lead for miles through lodgepole pine forest or across open sagebrush hills or grasslands—pleasant if time is no problem, but without the intricacies, unexpected views, and dramatic scenery that characterize trails in other regions. Yet in Yellowstone, as anywhere, the way to sense fully the dynamics of the land is to belong intimately for a time: to hike or ride, or canoe. Here, destinations should be picked with special care. Saddle horses for guided half-day and day rides are available mainly at Roosevelt-Tower Junction; for a list of wranglers providing pack trips, contact the park superintendent. Each visitor center has maps and detailed information concerning trails in that district. Ask about special attractions and current trail conditions, whether riding or hiking.

Bears: Hikers and bears actually have a good record of compatibility, but the potential for serious trouble cannot be overlooked. Certain precautions are called for, especially in grizzly country. Check with park rangers as to where bears have recently been sighted or seemed bothersome—and then plan on taking a different trail. Walk in the open rather than through brushy areas such as streamside willows, and be noisy. Talk, whistle, sing, fasten a bell to belt or pack, or a rattle made of a can with pebbles inside. Given a chance, bears stay out of men's way; the noise forewarns them and lets them move on.

Detour if a bear is sighted, particularly a grizzly. Stay upwind. Large parties and horse parties are seldom bothered; individual hikers or small groups seem the most vulnerable. Dogs particularly incite bears (and they are forbidden on park trails in any case, because of their disturbance to wildlife). Women should forgo cosmetics, perfumes, and hair spray in the back country; there is evidence that their odors irritate bears. Similarly, there is some indication that hiking while menstruating may not be wise.

Avoid hiking at night in grizzly country, and never sleep in clothes worn for cooking. Place sleeping bags at least three hundred feet from the cooking area and food cache. Choose dehydrated foods in preference to aromatic

Lodgepole pine forest

ones such as ham or bacon. Burn cans and food scraps to destroy odor, and gather the residue into plastic bags to pack out. Never leave such waste in the back country, not even buried. It will be dug up by animals and scattered. Be careful about pouring cooking liquids, especially fats, onto the ground; their odor may attract bears. Food should be suspended at least ten feet above the ground, dangling free from a branch or from a rope tied between two trees.

Try to avoid crowding a bear's sense of proper distance by staying at least one or two hundred feet away. If suddenly confronted at close range, don't run or move toward the bear. Stand still, speak in a soft monotone, and pick a tree to climb (black bears can climb trees, but adult grizzlies cannot). If the bear starts to come closer, drop a camera or a sweater as a momentary diversion, and head for the tree. If that fails, play dead. Never try to outrun a bear; it cannot be done unless the bear permits it, and it usually has the opposite effect of heightening fury. Instead of running, lie curled with knees drawn to chest and hands clasped over the back of the neck; do not scream or show panic. Grizzlies have ignored people lying in this position, or given a mere slap and gone on.

General precautions: Afternoon thunderstorms are frequent in summer, making rain gear essential. Be sure to stay off the peaks and ridges and away from lone trees if there is lightning. Winds sometimes come up suddenly and they can jump in mere minutes from thirty to sixty miles per hour, with gusts to ninety. Freezing temperatures are frequent at night, so sleeping bags should be warm. Preventative measures against sunburn are wise, since at Yellowstone's high elevations the sun's rays are intense. Mosquitos and horseflies often call for the best possible preventative—plus philosophical forbearance. For an extensive hike, carry a topographical map and compass and know how to use both. Let someone know your plans, and check back with him on your return. Get a fire permit (free at any ranger station). Remember that sinter crusts may be thin and easily broken, damaging thermal features and causing possible serious injury.

Naturalist-led hikes: An ideal way to sample what lies beyond the road is to join the walks led by ranger-naturalists in summer. Printed schedules, distances, and destinations are posted on bulletin boards or available at any visitor center. Trips range from an hour or two to all-day expeditions with everybody carrying his own lunch. Those preferring to explore on their own instead of in a group should also consult the schedules—then go to the same places at a different time. The conducted hikes have been picked to sample Yellowstone's finest, most accessible back country, so the suggestions are useful individually as well as when joining the group.

MAMMOTH AREA

MACMINN BENCH, on the lower slopes of Mount Everts, offers one of the wildlife spectacles of the continent, especially from October into June.

Bighorn sheep

Early morning or late afternoon is best. Bands of bighorn sheep numbering fifty or more graze the slopes, undisturbed by the patient, slow approach of a man. Antelope are usual, too, but are extremely wary. Deer can be expected, and elk often cross the bench. Coyotes check around the edges of the herds, watching for possible meals. There is no trail, but the slopes are open and easy to cross. Begin at the footbridge crossing the Gardner River half a mile inside the north entrance gate, or from the parking pullout next to the sign marking the forty-fifth parallel of latitude (2 miles toward Mammoth from the entrance gate). Allow about half an hour to climb onto the bench; then stroll and look for as long as time permits. By checking the slopes with binoculars in advance, one can locate the herds and decide on an approach route. A much longer alternative version of this hike is to the crest of MOUNT EVERTS and then eastward to Lava Creek. There are splendid mountain views from both the bench and the crest.

ELECTRIC PEAK (10,992 feet) lifts its summit higher than any other in the Gallatin Range. The approach is from Swan Lake Flat, above Mammoth. Follow the trail to CACHE LAKE (about 7 miles; a gentle rise through open country); then climb by the open ridge west of the lake (about 3 miles to the top with a three-thousand-foot elevation gain). There is no technical difficulty, but watch your footing on the last scramble to the top. A spur presents a knife edge with what appears to be a blank face after a way; drop around it to the left and climb up a rock chute to the summit. The view is across country well above treeline, with many rugged rock peaks both near and far, and forested country below.

Other high-country hikes in the Gallatin corner of the park—all fairly lengthy expeditions—include the following. Skirt along the summit ridge between JOSEPH PEAK (10,494 feet) and GRAY PEAK (10,292 feet), a little over a mile between the two summits with an additional 3 or 4 miles of cross-country hiking between the Sportsman Lake Trail and the Fawn Pass Trail, if a loop is desired. At Fawn Creek there is usually good fishing, and this is a pleasant hike in itself, but keep watch for grizzlies. From the Indian Creek Campground follow the trail to BIGHORN PASS (about 10 miles and two thousand feet gain in elevation). Bighorn rams may be seen in summer; elk are sure, and grizzly bears likely. There are several lakes, none good for fishing. If time and energy permit, follow the ridges north to BANNOCK PEAK (about 4 or 5 miles) or on to FAWN PASS (around 10 miles). Route finding is easy; the country is above treeline most of the way. Fawn Pass is particularly favored by grizzlies; twenty-two bears were counted there within a two- or three-mile radius during one wildlife survey.

Most hikes in the Gallatin Mountains can be approached from the west as easily as from the Mammoth side, and hikes to the petrified forests of SPECIMEN CREEK and DALY CREEK are in the extreme northwest corner of the park, accessible from U.S. 191. The slopes are steep, however, and the trees are difficult to find. (See the Specimen Ridge hike in the Northern section of this chapter for a more feasible petrified forest trail.)

WEST SIDE

FAIRY FALLS is reached by a 3-mile trail leaving from the Fountain Flat Road. It crosses a wet meadow much of the way and is quite level going. The falls drop into a pool in a forested setting. IMPERIAL GEYSER is on the hill about one mile farther; it plays sporadically, reaching to 125 feet. SPRAY GEYSER is close by. Lone buffalo bulls are sometimes seen on this hike.

MONUMENT BASIN perches on a ridge across the road from Artists Paint Pots (south of Norris). The trail is only about a mile long, but climbs 700 feet in its last half mile, and is quite steep. Monument Geyser sprays from a cylindrical cone eight feet high, and several smaller cones are grouped near by. SYLVAN SPRINGS lies at the base of the ridge north of Monument Geyser Basin. Its steam can be seen from the road, pinpointing the location, and the springs are reached by walking along the river bank from the road, skirting the meadow (which is too wet for pleasant travel until midsummer). After the Hebgen earthquake the springs became boiling and violent and so sulphurous that cones fallen from the trees into the water quickly became coated with yellow. Crusts here are fragile; be extremely cautious.

THE NORTHERN PARK

For a lengthy riverside hike (about 20 miles) follow the YELLOWSTONE RIVER from Hellroaring Creek to the town of Gardiner (cross the Yellowstone by the suspension bridge east of Hellroaring Creek). The trail is gentle with excellent campsites along the way. This is a hot hike in summer, but ideal in spring or fall. Bighorn, antelope, elk, and buffalo are common in spring.

The easiest approach to the PETRIFIED FOREST on Specimen Ridge is by following the west fork of Crystal Creek, reached by the spur road off the Lamar Valley road (about 6 miles from Tower Junction). Allow at least half a day; the roundtrip distance is not over 4 or 5 miles, but the ridge rises steeply and finding the tree specimens takes time. Carry water. (A naturalist-led walk also goes here.) Three standing petrified stumps can be seen with binoculars from the first roadside pullout west of Crystal Creek. They are high on the ridge, just above the east edge of a bare cliff. One appears as broad as it is high, and the others are taller and more slender. The largest stump, five feet across, has a hollow center filled with earth that supports a small garden of flowers. The stone itself is vivid with red, black, and gray lichen. The stumps close by stand at least ten feet high, and others are visible in the forest below, screened and brushed by the branches of living Douglas firs. (Reminder: collecting specimens is illegal, irresponsible, and subject to severe penalty.)

In the SLOUGH CREEK area, the hill above the campground offers a beautiful short walk at sunset or sunrise. The way leads through forest to an open hilltop with a sweeping view of the Lamar Valley. In summer, ten or twelve species of flowers can be seen even with a casual look. The fishermen's path along the creek is also worth sampling, with or without rod in hand. Or, for a longer hike, follow the old wagon road and trail that starts

Slough Creek

up the hill about half a mile south of the campground. After 2 miles of gentle climbing it breaks out of the trees into a green valley with Slough Creek meandering through and dramatic peaks showing beyond. Watch for moose. This trail is ideal for an early morning hike combined with fishing.

For a close feeling of mountains from the shelter of a valley try the PEBBLE CREEK hike beginning at the trailhead a mile inside the northeast entrance gate. It climbs steeply for a mile or two, then enters the head of a cirquelike valley with green meadows, offering a chance to see elk, moose, and perhaps bighorn on the cliffs, and good cutthroat trout fishing. (The fish are small in the upper valley, but bigger farther downstream.) Abiathar Peak and Amphitheater Mountain are prominent on the hike into the valley, and Cutoff Peak (10,638 feet) stands at the head of the valley. If time and transportation permit, follow the valley down to the Pebble Creek Campground (about 11 miles from the head of the valley).

A forested hike leads up the Cache Creek Trail and then cross-country to THE NEEDLE (about 13 miles). Instead of a spire, the "needle" is a needle's eye, an arch thirty or forty feet high cutting through the crest of a rock ridge. The last 2 or 3 miles require brush whacking through a spruce and fir forest. For a longer hike (or a horse trip), leave from the same point near Soda Butte and follow the Lamar River Trail to its end (nearly 30 miles) and then go about 7 miles beyond to the HOODOO BASIN. Here the breccia walls of a basin half a mile long have eroded into grotesque "hoodoos" thirty feet high.

CANYON

THE SEVEN-MILE-HOLE trail leaves the road from the Glacial Boulder, near Inspiration Point. It follows the rim of the canyon, offering a fine view of SILVER CORD CASCADE after 1.5 miles; then in another 1.5 miles it drops abruptly to the river, a spectacular 1,250-foot descent—and a grueling climb back out. Fishing is excellent, especially after the first high water of the summer has gone; cutthroat run twelve to fourteen inches.

Another descent into the canyon is via UNCLE TOMS TRAIL, a series of walkways and stairs leading from the south rim part way to the base of the Lower Falls. From this viewpoint the true height and force of this falls can be appreciated—aspects not fully realized from the rim because of the awesome scale of the canyon as a whole. On cold days or early mornings there may be ice; be careful with footing. A plastic bag to protect cameras or binoculars may be advisable, depending on where the mist is blowing. Grass and moss and ferns on the walls close to the plunge pool of the falls testify to the dampness. The walls directly at the base of the falls are probably even more thickly upholstered, but the spray makes it impossible to see. The hike is short, hard on legs and lungs, and thoroughly rewarding for anyone in good health and willing to exert a bit (including young children), but too tiring, or even dangerous, for anyone who is frail or has heart trouble.

The RED ROCK POINT TRAIL, descending from Lookout Point on the North Rim, also provides a superlative view of the Lower Falls and the canyon. This trail, too, is steep but it is shorter than the Seven-Mile-Hole and Uncle Toms trails.

From Artist Point a one-mile trail winds along the rim to POINT SUB-LIME, a favorite canyon viewpoint.

For mountain hikes in the Canyon area, try OBSERVATION PEAK (9,397 feet) in the Washburn Mountains. Allow all day; the hike is about 6 miles one way. Topography is varied with meadows, lodgepole pine forests, open hillsides, and spruce and fir forests. The view sweeps the central reaches of the park, living up to its name.

EAST SIDE

MOUNT WASHBURN makes a fine destination for a hike, especially via the trail from Dunraven Pass (about 3.5 miles). The peak stands isolated, and the view is perhaps the most sweeping in the park. Hayden Valley stretches southward to Yellowstone Lake, and the awesome gash of the Canyon shows as a mere tear in the forested expanse of Mirror Plateau. Close by, flowers mantle the slopes in summer; moose may be seen, and bighorn sheep are likely near the mountaintop. Watch also for glacial scratches near the summit, grooves caused as ice eight hundred feet thick rasped against the mountainside.

Indian paintbrush

Ask about the approach to JONES PASS for a sample of the Absaroka crest. Leave from a service road near Lake Butte or by working cross-country. Flowers are exceptionally fine, usually by late July. Carry water or count on using snow, which usually lingers into late August. There is no regularly maintained trail. Another mountain hike is to AVALANCHE PEAK, near Sylvan Pass, leaving from the first parking area west of Lake Eleanor. This is a steep 2-mile climb through subalpine meadows to true alpine conditions on top. Flowers are superb. The view is dominated by the lake, with all of the arms showing plainly. Beyond, the Teton Range shows to the south, and to the west and north the view stretches into Idaho and Montana. An avalanche area lies about one-third of the way up. Stumps four and five feet high, sheared off as snow roared downslope, can be seen. Use caution in crossing the talus near the top. Notice the route carefully as there is no regular trail.

THE SOUTHERN PARK

HEART LAKE lies about 8 miles by trail at the base of Mount Sheridan, with Witch Creek thermal basin and Rustic Geyser along its western shore. Most of the way is gently rolling country, through lodgepole, with no steep climbs except the short drop down Witch Creek to the lake. The view from Mount Sheridan includes the Tetons and Pitchstone Plateau, as well as Yellowstone Lake and, of course, Heart Lake. Lake trout are large here, hard to catch but a satisfying challenge. Across the road from the Heart Lake trailhead is the shortest SHOSHONE LAKE trail (4 miles from Dogshead Creek, through the forest, to the lake's outlet into the Lewis River). A more scenic hike to Shoshone Lake begins near Old Faithful and follows along the Firehole River, then over Grants Pass (where a spring just south of the pass makes an excellent lunch spot). The lake is reached in about 7 miles via a final spur trail branching from SHOSHONE GEYSER BASIN, just over the hill from the lake. The basin gives a chance to have a "private" thermal area of considerable size and variety. Geysers spout skyward, and hot springs boil over into the river, turning short stretches just the right temperature for swimming. Hot springs also warm shallow water along the edge of the lake. Another approach to Shoshone Lake is down DeLacy Creek from a trailhead 3 miles east of Craig Pass, on the road from Old Faithful to West Thumb. This trail follows the meanders of the creek to a swampy meadow at the lakeshore, about 4 miles. There is a fine display of wildflowers in early summer along the creek, and brook trout fishing.

If transportation can be arranged, try the 18-mile hike through BECHLER CANYON (beyond Shoshone Lake in the extreme southwest corner of the park, its southern end accessible by road only via Ashton, Idaho). This part of Yellowstone gets the heaviest snowfall, resulting in luxuriant vegetation and the constant music of running water. Waterfalls leap within sight and sound of one another, each with its own charm. Colonnade Falls is a repeti-

Lewis River

tion of itself, with twin plunges about one hundred feet apart. Iris Falls tumbles over a stone lip twice as broad as it is high. Three-River Junction and Ragged Falls are in a deep canyon setting, luxurious with fern and abundant splashing water. Prowl around to find all the falls shown on the contour maps and also the hot springs, which are not spectacular to the eye but are a joy for a leisurely wilderness bath.

The THOROFARE AREA perhaps symbolizes the Yellowstone wilderness better than any other section of the park. Ideal for a saddle trip, it offers 45 miles of trail through roadless country, and several approach points make it feasible for hikers as well as riders. The way threads forests and meadows, leading around the south and east sides of Yellowstone Lake past a scattering of small lakes and hot springs. Wildlife is all but guaranteed. Access points are from the south entrance, the Heart Lake Trail, or from a trailhead about 17 miles inside the east entrance of the park. High water in creeks spilling out of the Absaroka Mountains makes the northern Thorofare exceedingly wet for travel in spring and early summer, even on horseback, but from mid-July into autumn it is wild country at its best, registering deeply on eye and heart and weaving itself forever into the fabric of the inner being.

BOAT TRIPS

Motor Boats: Rowboats, outboard skiffs, and cruisers can be rented at Bridge Bay and Grant Village. Free launch ramps are at the same locations, and also east of Steamboat Point (on the north shore of Yellowstone Lake) and at the Lewis Lake Campground.

Boating facilitates fishing and exploring the lakes—including the islands of Yellowstone Lake—whether for day trips or longer. Lake camp trips make ideal away-from-it-all experiences for those who are equipped and self-sufficient. Beaches on the far shore of LEWIS LAKE (about 3 miles across) offer picnic sites, and the FLAT MOUNTAIN ARM of Yellowstone Lake is a particular gem. It is about 12 miles from West Thumb to the beginning of Flat Mountain Arm, and another 4 miles to its upper end. Best camping is among the coves and bars in the middle section of the south shore of Flat Mountain Arm. The extreme tip is shallow and marshy, a haven for waterbirds. Prevailing winds funnel up the arm and raise the water from choppiness to waves every afternoon, so plans should be made accordingly.

Canoes, Kayaks, Rowboats: Escape beyond the sound (and convenience) of motors is possible in the SOUTH and SOUTHEAST ARMS of Yellowstone Lake and on Shoshone Lake. (Verify current restrictions.) These waters are open only to hand-propelled craft. The upper arms of Yellowstone Lake abound in birds, moose, flower fields, and features of geologic interest. Sloughs and fingering channels invite exploration in the upper end of South Arm and at Chipmunk Creek. From the creek, a portage to Southeast Arm is feasible. It is less than a mile of fairly level travel and often preferable to the alternative of paddling the east shore, which is vulnerable to afternoon wind. Watch for ospreys fishing on the delta of the Yellowstone River, and for bull elk herding their harems in late summer. Camping is permitted only at designated sites; check availability ahead of time at Lake Ranger Station.

Moose staying cool at midday

A problem with the arms of upper Yellowstone Lake is getting there. Their mouths require an extremely long paddle around the shoreline from West Thumb, and, for safety, travel always should be close to shore, not across open water. A two-to-five-horsepower outboard motor can be mounted on a canoe or rowboat and used to shorten the miles to the beginning of the restricted waters, then stowed in favor of paddles or oars; or a tow can be arranged through the concessioner on the lake (but this is costly). With time enough, the distance is no problem. Simply plan to paddle early in the morning and after the midday blow has calmed—usually before 11:00 A.M. and after somewhere between 4:00 and 7:00 P.M. Smooth water or a gentle following wind permit two paddlers to make a comfortable three or four miles per hour. Consequently, a week is a minimum time for a trip to the upper lake, paddling all the way; ten days to two weeks is far better, allowing time to search out side waterways, to explore and observe and savor. Each arm is about 10 miles long.

SHOSHONE LAKE offers much the same charm as South Arm and Southeast Arm, and can be explored in a shorter time. Even one long day will permit a sample, and three days to a week is ample time. Launch at Lewis Lake; cross to its northwest end (about 2 miles); then paddle up the Lewis River. The last mile gets too shallow and swift for paddling but can easily be waded, with the laden canoe pulled along by the painter. The total length of the river is 3 miles. Shoshone Lake stretches for about 10 miles from the head of the river, with an intricate shoreline of sloughs to paddle into and bluffs to climb. There are brown, lake, and eastern brook trout to catch, moose to watch for along the shore, and a geyser basin at the upper end of the lake to explore. Here the bubbling of a small, lakeshore hot spring merges with the slap of waves to furnish an unusual all-night lullaby. In summer weeks when visitors to the park number more than forty thousand per day, the lake and the geyser basin provide solitude as well as the particular sort of fascination and beauty that characterize Yellowstone.

For all back-country water trips, write ahead for information or check current regulations and conditions at any ranger station or visitor center. (If necessary, pursue the question until someone sufficiently knowledgeable is found; not every uniformed person can be expected to have full personal knowledge of each part of the back country in so vast a park as Yellowstone.) All boats must have a permit, obtainable at most ranger stations. Fire permits are also needed for camping. Both permits are issued only in person, not by mail, because the contact gives a chance to pass on information and to encourage wise use of the wilderness—to foster an attitude of cherishing and safeguarding which both enhances the present trip and insures the chance of future trips for generations to come. The primeval quality of Yellowstone is a legacy from the past, held in trust today, for the tomorrows yet to come.

INDEX

Numbers in italics refer to illustrations.

Maps

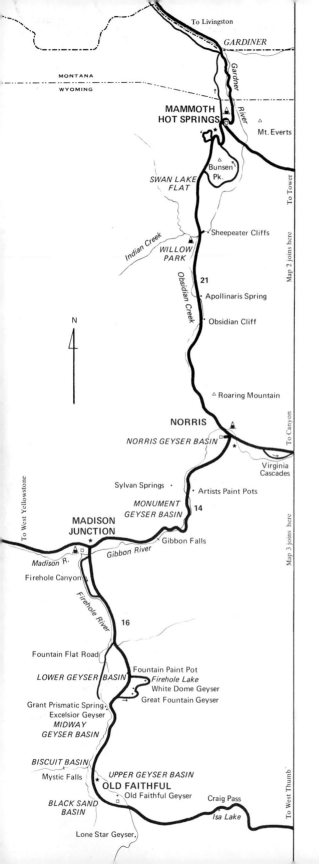

POINTS OF INTEREST

The hot spring terraces at MAMMOTH, across SWAN LAKE FLAT and WILLOW PARK, past OBSIDIAN CLIFF and ROARING MOUNTAIN; then along the GIBBON and FIREHOLE RIVERS to NORRIS, LOWER, MIDWAY, and UPPER GEYSER BASINS. Several short, relatively quiet side roads invite exploration and lingering; trails and boardwalks lead through the thermal basins. Museum displays and audiovisual programs are located at Mammoth, Norris, Madison, and Old Faithful.

WILDLIFE POSSIBILITIES

Antelope can usually be seen the year around near Mammoth in the Stephens Creek and MacMinn Bench areas. Mule deer congregate in the same general area, especially in winter, and bighorn sheep are easily seen in fall, winter, and spring. Moose feed in the soggy wetness of Willow Park, particu-

VISITOR CENTER	□
CAMPGROUND	▲
ROAD	▬
MILEAGE	★ 14 ★

0 1 2 3 4 5
Miles

MAP 1
THERMAL BASINS

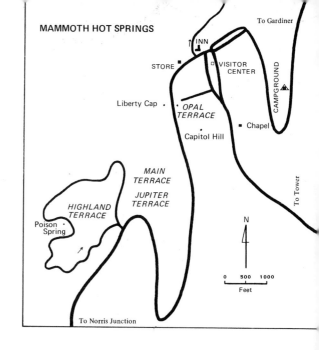

larly in the early morning and at dusk. Sandhill cranes court and trumpet their wild music along the meadows of Obsidian Creek. Elk frequent the region of the Gibbon and Firehole rivers the year around, and Canada geese graze these same rich green meadows and river banks. In summer buffalo shift to high ranges, but the rest of the year they add to the wildlife scene along the Firehole River. Marmots bound through the rocks and sound their shrill call from the hilltop observation point above Old Faithful.

GEYSER ERUPTION TABLE

Check at visitor centers for current information and for the time of the last eruption of major geysers. From this, some idea of what to expect is possible—but it is only a guess based on statistical averages. In actuality each geyser follows its individual timetable, depending on the exact circumstances of the moment.

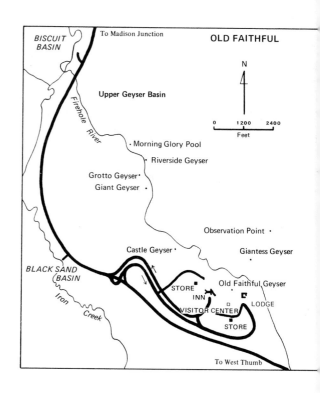

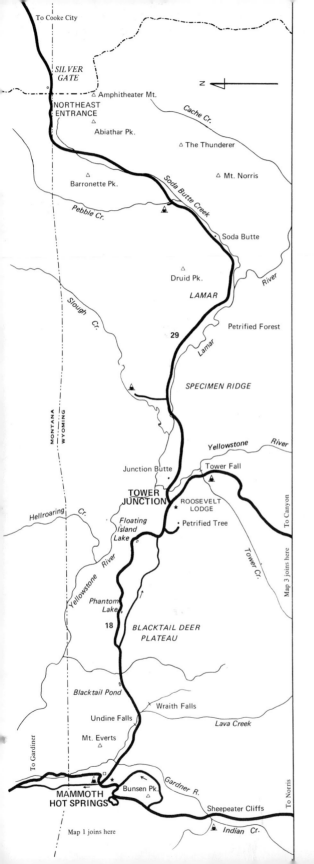

POINTS OF INTEREST

The old FORT YELLOWSTONE buildings at MAMMOTH, now used as headquarters for the National Park Service; across sagebrush flats, past waterfalls and ponds to a petrified tree; then out the LAMAR VALLEY to the mountainous northeast corner of the park. This is one of the least-frequented portions of Yellowstone, probably because it has no significant thermal areas or spectacular features such as Yellowstone Lake or the Canyon of the Yellowstone River; but the drive gives a great sense of the openness and wildness characteristic of the park interior beyond the reach of roads.

WILDLIFE POSSIBILITIES

Bighorn sheep are common on the cliffs of Mount Everts and of Junction Butte and Mount Norris in Lamar Valley. Ducks, teals, and coots paddle on small ponds, and redwing blackbirds warble from the marshy shores. Mule deer are frequent; so are coyotes feeding on winterkill elk carcasses or looking along the roadside for pocket gophers. At night headlights may catch the eyeshine of a bobcat. Lone moose sometimes roam near Mammoth, in the Lava Creek–Wraith Falls vicinity, and throughout Lamar Valley. Antelope are fairly frequent in the valley during the summer, and buffalo are almost certain to be found from late fall through May in lower Lamar Valley and around Junction Butte. Cliff swallows nest in a large colony on the side of Soda Butte.

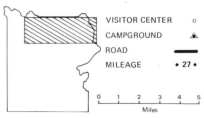

VISITOR CENTER	□
CAMPGROUND	▲
ROAD	
MILEAGE	★ 27 ★

0 1 2 3 4 5
Miles

MAP 2
THE NORTHERN PARK

POINTS OF INTEREST

The NARROWS of the canyon near Tower Junction, and TOWER FALLS a short way beyond; then over the high slopes of MOUNT WASHBURN, through the flower fields of DUNRAVEN PASS, and on to the GRAND CANYON OF THE YELLOWSTONE; from there, through HAYDEN VALLEY and past MUD VOLCANO.

WILDLIFE POSSIBILITIES

A band of bighorn sheep usually summers on Mount Washburn; pikas, marmots, and red squirrels are also frequently found. Bears are seen along the roads. (Do not create a traffic jam by stopping to watch them, and, for the sake of both man and bear, do not feed them.) Osprey dive after fish in the bottom of the Canyon, and nest on the tops of rock pinnacles upthrust from the walls. They build disordered piles of sticks as much as three feet in diameter and return year after year to the same nest, simply refurbishing the tangle by adding more sticks. Through Hayden Valley, watch for lone buffalo bulls, moose, elk, and deer during the summer; also for herds of buffalo from October until mid-June. Grizzly bears are occasionally seen on the distant hills, digging for pocket gophers and roots, and there may be coyotes trotting along the river banks or across the slopes. Along the river, Canada geese feed the year around; watch, too, for swans, pelicans, and a host of other waterbirds.

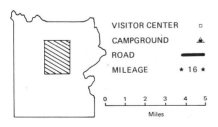

VISITOR CENTER	□
CAMPGROUND	⛺
ROAD	▬▬
MILEAGE	★ 16 ★

0 1 2 3 4 5
Miles

**MAP 3
CANYON**

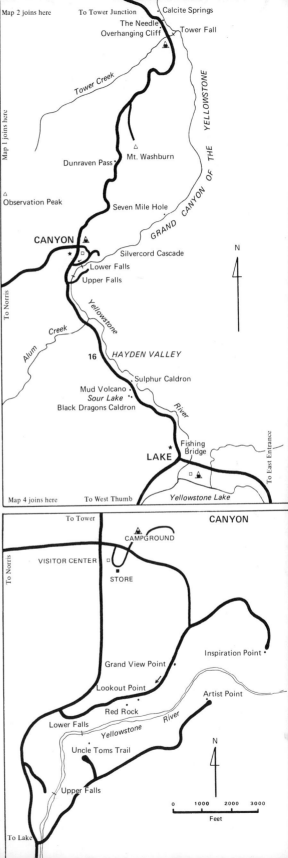

Map 2 joins here · To Tower Junction · Calcite Springs
The Needle
Overhanging Cliff · Tower Fall
Tower Creek
Map 1 joins here
GRAND CANYON OF THE YELLOWSTONE
Dunraven Pass · △ Mt. Washburn
△ Observation Peak
Seven Mile Hole
CANYON ⛺
Silvercord Cascade
Lower Falls
Upper Falls
To Norris
Alum Creek
Yellowstone
16 · HAYDEN VALLEY
Sulphur Caldron
Mud Volcano
Sour Lake
Black Dragons Caldron
River
Fishing Bridge
LAKE
To East Entrance
Map 4 joins here · To West Thumb · Yellowstone Lake

N

CANYON
To Tower
⛺ CAMPGROUND
VISITOR CENTER
To Norris
STORE
Inspiration Point ·
Grand View Point ·
Lookout Point
Artist Point
Red Rock
Lower Falls
Yellowstone River
Uncle Toms Trail
N
Upper Falls
To Lake

0 1000 2000 3000
Feet

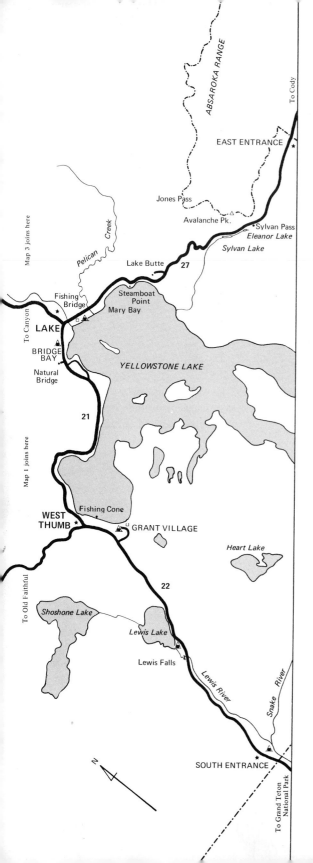

POINTS OF INTEREST

Around the north shore of YEL-LOWSTONE LAKE to SYLVAN PASS; also along the west shore of the lake, including the thermal basin at WEST THUMB, then south to LEWIS LAKE and the South Entrance of the Park. There are visitor centers with displays and programs at Fishing Bridge and Grant Village.

WILDLIFE POSSIBILITIES

Cutthroat trout spawn from late June to mid-July at Mary Bay, on the north shore of the Lake, and also in the Yellowstone River—a sight of fecundity and the ongoing thrust of life. Waterbirds abound on Yellowstone Lake, and shore-birds stalk the beaches, probing with long bills for larvae and crustaceans. At Sylvan Pass, pikas and marmots live in the talus, sounding their high-pitched whistles from lookout posts and tunnel entrances.

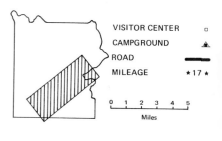

VISITOR CENTER	□
CAMPGROUND	▲
ROAD	▬
MILEAGE	★17★

0 1 2 3 4 5
Miles

MAP 4
YELLOWSTONE LAKE AREA

DIRECTORY

CAMPING facilities inside the park operate at full capacity during the summer season, with all permissible camp sites filling by as early as mid-day. Most campgrounds are open from early June to mid-September; Mammoth Hot Springs stays open the year around. Use regulations and fees vary from year to year according to congressional directives; check current status. Additional campgrounds are available outside the park on National Forest land and also under private ownership. Major campgrounds inside the park include those at Bridge Bay, Canyon, Fishing Bridge, Grant Village, Madison, and Norris. These are in settings of lodgepole pine in overall flat areas; they are large and efficient. Of moderate size and situated on more varied terrain are the campgrounds at Indian Creek, Lewis Lake, Mammoth, and Tower. Smaller still and more intimate are those at Pebble Creek, Slough Creek, and Snake River. *Water, sewer,* and *power hookups* are available at the concession-operated campground at Fishing Bridge. *Dump stations* for trailer holding tanks are at Bridge Bay, Canyon, Fishing Bridge, Grant Village, Madison, and Old Faithful. *Propane gas* is usually available from service stations at Fishing Bridge, Grant Village, and Old Faithful. *Showers* are at Canyon Village, Fishing Bridge, Grant Village, Lake, Mammoth, and Old Faithful; *laundromats* are at the same locations, except that there are none at Mammoth.

ACCOMMODATIONS range from modestly luxurious cabins and hotel rooms to simple shelters with minimal furnishings and budget prices. All are operated by the Yellowstone Park Company (*address* Yellowstone Park Company, Yellowstone National Park, Wyoming 82190). *Inns* are at Mammoth, Lake, and Old Faithful; *cabins* (deluxe to economy) at Canyon Village, Fishing Bridge, Lake, Mammoth, Roosevelt, and Old Faithful.

MEAL SERVICE, including dining rooms, cafeterias, and snack bars, is available at Canyon, Fishing Bridge, Lake, Mammoth, Old Faithful, Roosevelt, and West Thumb.

STORES selling groceries, drug items, film, fishing tackle, and souvenirs are at Canyon Village, Fishing Bridge, Lake, Mammoth, Old Faithful, Roosevelt, Tower Falls, and West Thumb.

GASOLINE STATIONS are at Canyon, Fishing Bridge, Grant Village, Lake, Mammoth, Old Faithful, Tower Junction, and West Thumb.

MEDICAL SERVICES are obtainable from well-staffed clinics at Lake and Mammoth, and from nurses stationed at Old Faithful and West Thumb. In an emergency, ask for help at any ranger station.

TELEPHONES are at all developed areas, including most campgrounds.

POST OFFICES: Canyon, Lake, Mammoth, and Old Faithful.

ACTIVITIES range from *saddle trips, stagecoach rides,* and *cookouts* (centered at Roosevelt, near Tower Junction) to various motor coach *sightseeing trips* and *boat excursions* operated by the Yellowstone Park Company (write for current schedules and prices). The naturalist program of the National Park Service offers free naturalist-led *hikes,* plus visitor center and outdoor *campfire programs* (see posted schedules). *Boats* are rented at Bridge Bay and Grant Village; *launch ramps* are at Bridge Bay, Grant Village, Lewis Lake, and east of Steamboat Point. Check regarding current *fishing* regulations.

INFORMATION: Address the Superintendent, Yellowstone National Park, Wyoming 82190. To purchase books and maps, write the Yellowstone Library and Museum Association, Yellowstone National Park, Wyoming 82190.